Collected Poems

1951–1971

By A. R. Ammons

Ommateum

Expressions of Sea Level

Corsons Inlet

Tape for the Turn of the Year

Northfield Poems

Selected Poems

Uplands

Briefings

Collected Poems: 1951–1971
(winner of the National Book Award for Poetry, 1973)

Sphere: The Form of a Motion
(winner of the 1973–1974 Bollingen Prize in Poetry)

Diversifications

The Snow Poems

Highgate Roate

The Selected Poems: 1951–1977

Selected Longer Poems

A Coast of Trees
(winner of the National Book Critics Circle Award for Poetry, 1981)

Worldly Hopes

Lake Effect Country

The Selected Poems: Expanded Edition

Sumerian Vistas

The Really Short Poems

Garbage
(winner of the National Book Award for Poetry, 1993)

Brink Road

Glare

Collected Poems

1951-1971

●●

A. R. AMMONS

WITHDRAWN

W. W. Norton & Company

NEW YORK • LONDON

First published as a Norton paperback 2001

For information about permission to reproduce selections from this
book, write to Permissions, W. W. Norton & Company, Inc.,
500 Fifth Avenue, New York, NY 10110

Printed in the United States of America

Library of Congress Cataloging-in-Publication Data

Ammons, A. R., 1926–
Collected Poems, 1951–1971.
PS3501.M6A17 1972 811'.5'4 72-5811
ISBN 0-393-04241-3
ISBN 0-393-32192-4 pbk.

W. W. Norton & Company, Inc.,
500 Fifth Avenue, New York, N.Y. 10110
www.wwnorton.com

W. W. Norton & Company Ltd.,
Castle House, 75/76 Wells St., London, W1T 3QT

1 2 3 4 5 6 7 8 9 0

To the memory of my mother and father

Acknowledgments

I am grateful to the editors of the following periodicals for first publishing the poems listed:

Abraxas: "Left," "Mid-August," "Path," "The Fall."
Contemporary Poets of South Jersey: "Ocean City."
Epoch: "Fall Creek," "Rectitude."
Epos: "Event," "Look for my White Self," "This Black Rich Country."
Foxfire: "Trouble Making Trouble" (formerly, "Front").
Harper's: "One More Time," "Terminus," "The Eternal City."
The Hudson Review: "Christmas Eve," "Essay on Poetics."
Lillabulero: "Day," "Definitions," "Delaware Water Gap," "Ground Tide," "High Surreal," "Sorting," "Translating."
Modern Occasions: "The City Limits," "Triphammer Bridge."
The Nation: "Timing."
New American Review: "The Arc Inside and Out."
The New York Times: "Communication."

The following publishers have kindly granted me permission to reprint poems from the cited books:

Dorrance & Co.: *Ommateum*, 1955.
Ohio State University Press: *Expressions of Sea Level*, 1964.
Cornell University Press: *Corsons Inlet*, 1965; *Northfield Poems*, 1966.
W. W. Norton & Co., Inc.: *Uplands*, 1970; *Briefings*, 1971.

"Grace Abounding" first appeared in *Beyond the Square—A Tribute to Elliott Coleman*, edited by Robert K. Rosenberg.

Special thanks are due to the Creative Artists Public Service Program of the Cultural Council Foundation (New York State) for a grant which enabled me to spend the summer of 1971 preparing this volume.

I must acknowledge—if in some cases re-acknowledge—a sense of the continuous presence of certain people who have been necessary to my life and work: Josephine Miles, Frederick Morgan, John Logan, Josephine Jacobsen, Elliott Coleman, Milton Kessler, David Ray, Baxter Hathaway, Bernhard Kendler, Richard Howard, Harold Bloom. My sisters, Vida Cox and Mona Smith, have from the beginning of my writing sustained me unfailingly. In the love of my wife, Phyllis, and my son, John, I know the source of these poems.

Contents

Contents

Contents

Contents

Collected Poems

1951–1971

So I Said I Am Ezra

So I said I am Ezra
and the wind whipped my throat
gaming for the sounds of my voice
   I listened to the wind
go over my head and up into the night
Turning to the sea I said
       I am Ezra
but there were no echoes from the waves
The words were swallowed up
   in the voice of the surf
or leaping over the swells
lost themselves oceanward
   Over the bleached and broken fields
I moved my feet and turning from the wind
   that ripped sheets of sand
   from the beach and threw them
   like seamists across the dunes
swayed as if the wind were taking me away
and said
      I am Ezra
As a word too much repeated
falls out of being
so I Ezra went out into the night
like a drift of sand
and splashed among the windy oats
that clutch the dunes
of unremembered seas

The Sap Is Gone Out of the Trees

The sap is gone out of the trees
in the land of my birth
and the branches droop
   The rye is rusty in the fields
and the oatgrains are light in the wind
The combine sucks at the fields

and coughs out dry mottled straw
The bags of grain are chaffy and light

The oatfields said Oh
and Oh said the wheatfields as the dusting
combine passed over
and long after the dust was gone
   Oh they said
and looked around at the stubble and straw
The sap is gone out of the hollow straws
and the marrow out of my bones
                  They are
   brittle and dry
   and painful in this land

The wind whipped at my carcass saying
How shall I
   coming from these fields
water the fields of earth
   and I said Oh
   and fell down in the dust

In Strasbourg in 1349

In Strasbourg in 1349
in the summer and in the whole year
there went a plague through the earth
   Death walked on both sides of the Sea
tasting Christian and Saracen flesh
and took another turn about the Sea
In a black gown and scarlet cape she went
skipping across the Sea
freeing ships to rear and fly in the wind
   with their cargoes of dead
      Vultures whipped amorous wings
in the shadow of death
and death was happy with them and flew swiftly
whirling a lyrical dance on hidden feet
Dogs ate their masters' empty hands

and death going wild with joy
hurried about the Sea
and up the rivers to the mountains

The dying said
Damn us
the Jews have poisoned the wells
and death throwing her head about lifted
the skirts of her gown
and danced wildly

The rich Jews are burning on loose platforms
in 1349
and death jumps into the fire
setting the flames wild with her dancing

So I left and walked up into the air
and sat down in a cool draft
my face hot from watching the fire
When morning came
I looked down at the ashes
and rose and walked out of the world

I Broke a Sheaf of Light

I broke a sheaf of light
from a sunbeam
that was slipping through thunderheads
drawing a last vintage from the hills
O golden sheaf I said
and throwing it on my shoulder
brought it home to the corner
O very pretty light I said
and went out to my chores
The cow lowed from the pasture and I answered
yes I am late
already the evening star
The pigs heard me coming and squealed
From the stables a neigh reminded me

yes I am late having forgot
I have been out to the sunbeam
and broken a sheaf of gold
    Returning to my corner
I sat by the fire with the sheaf of light
that shone through the night
and was hardly gone when morning came

Some Months Ago

Some months ago I went out early
to pay
   my last respects to earth
          farewell earth
       ocean farewell
lean eucalyptus with nude gray skin
          farewell

   Hill rain
pouring from a rockpierced cloud
hill rain from the wounds of mist
        farewell

See the mountainpeaks gather
clouds from the sky
shake new bright flakes from the mist
        farewell

Hedgerows hung with web and dew
that disappear at a touch
   like snail eyes
        farewell
To a bird only this
        farewell
and he hopped away to peck dew
from a ground web
   spider running out of her tunnel to see
to whom I said

farewell
and she sat still on her heavy webs

I closed up all the natural throats of earth
and cut my ties with every natural heart
and saying farewell
   stepped out into the great open

Bees Stopped

Bees stopped on the rock
and rubbed their headparts and wings
rested then flew on:
ants ran over the whitish greenish reddish
plants that grow flat on rocks
and people never see
because nothing should grow on rocks:
I looked out over the lake
and beyond to the hills and trees
and nothing was moving
so I looked closely
along the lakeside
under the old leaves of rushes
and around clumps of drygrass
and life was everywhere
so I went on sometimes whistling

Rack

The pieces of my voice have been thrown
away I said turning to the hedgerows
and hidden ditches
Where do the pieces of
my voice lie scattered
The cedarcone said you have been ground
down into and whirled

Tomorrow I must go look under the clumps of
marshgrass in wet deserts

and in dry deserts
when the wind falls from the mountain
inquire of the chuckwalla what he saw go by
and what the sidewinder found
risen in the changing sand
I must run down all the pieces
and build the whole silence back

As I look across the fields the sun
big in my eyes I see the hills
the great black unwasting silence and
know I must go out beyond the hills and seek
for I am broken over the earth—
so little remains
for the silent offering of my death

Chaos Staggered Up the Hill

Chaos staggered up the hill
and got the daisies dirty
that were pretty along the road:
messy chaos I said
but then in cooler mind saw
incipient eyes revolving in it
with possibly incipient sorrow
and had to admire how
it got along at all
in its kind of weather:
passing, it engulfed me
and I couldn't know dissolving
it had rhizobia with it
to make us green some other place.

I Went Out to the Sun

I went out to the sun
where it burned over a desert willow

and getting under the shade of the willow
I said
   It's very hot in this country
The sun said nothing so I said
   The moon has been talking about you
and he said
   Well what is it this time

   She says it's her own light
He threw his flames out so far
they almost scorched the top of the willow
   Well I said of course I don't know

The sun went on and the willow was glad
I found an arroyo and dug for water
which I got muddy and then clear
so I drank a lot
and washed the salt from my eyes
and taking off my shirt
hung it on the willow to dry and said
   This land where whirlwinds
walking at noon in tall columns of dust
   take stately turns about the desert
   is a very dry land
So I went to sleep under the willow tree

When the moon came up it was cold
and reaching to the willow for my shirt
I said to the moon
   You make it a pretty night
so she smiled

A night-lizard rattled stems behind me
and the moon said
   I see over the mountain
   the sun is angry
Not able to see him I called and said
   Why are you angry with the moon
   since all at last must be lost
   to the great vacuity

Consignee

I have been brought out of day,
out of the full dawn led away;
    from the platform of noon
I have descended.

To death, the diffuse one
going beside me, I said,
    You have brought me out of day
and he said
No longer like the fields of earth
may you go in and out.

I quarreled and devised a while
    but went on
having sensed a nice dominion in the air,
the black so round and deep.

At Dawn in 1098

At dawn in 1098
the Turks went out from the gates
of Antioch
and gathered their dead
from the banks of the river
the cool ones
they gathered in

Bathing in the morning river
I said Oh
to the reapers
and stepping out gave
my white form to morning
She blushed openly
so twisting I danced
along the banks of the river
and morning rushed up over the hills

to see my wild form
whirling on the banks of the river
Saying O morning
I went away to the hills

With cloaks
and ornaments
arrows and coins of gold
the Turks buried their dead
and sealed the tombs with tears
But the Christians rising from the fields
broke open the cool tombs
and cut off heads
for a tally

Taking morning in my arms
I said Oh
and descended the eastern hills
and all that day
it was night in Antioch

The Whaleboat Struck

The whaleboat struck
and we came ashore
to the painted faces
   O primitives I said
and the arrow sang to my throat
Leaving myself on the shore
I went away
and when a heavy wind caught me I said
   My body lies south
    given over to vultures and flies
and wrung my hands
so the wind went on
Another day a wind came saying
   Bones
    lovely and white
    lie on the southern sand

      the ocean has washed bright
I said
      O bones in the sun
and went south
The flies were gone
The vultures no longer searched
the ends of my hingeless bones
for a trace of lean or gristle
Breathing the clean air
I picked up a rib
      to draw figures in the sand
till there is no roar in the ocean
no green in the sea
till the northwind flings no waves
across the open sea
I running in and out with the waves
I singing old Devonshire airs

Turning a Moment to Say So Long

      Turning a moment to say so long
            to the spoken
            and seen
            I stepped into
the implicit pausing sometimes
on the way to listen to unsaid things
At a boundary of mind
      Oh I said brushing up
      against the unseen
      and whirling on my heel
      said
   I have overheard too much
Peeling off my being I plunged into
the well
The fingers of the water splashed
            to grasp me up
            but finding only
            a few shafts
      of light

                too quick to grasp
                became hysterical
                jumped up and down
                    and wept copiously
        So I said I'm sorry dear well but
        went on deeper
        finding patched innertubes beer cans
        and black roothairs along the way
        but went on deeper
        till darkness snuffed the shafts of light
                against the well's side
                    night kissing
                the last bubbles from my lips

Turning

Turning from the waterhole I said Oh
to the lioness whose wrinkled forehead
showed signs of wonder
O beautiful relaxed animal I said
    The tall grass shivered up and down
and said
What a looseness is in her body how
limp are the wet teats of her belly
The grass sang a song I had never
    heard before to the red sun
so I said cool evening with a wind
in the rushes
The lioness dropped loosely to the ground
and I said O tired lioness
    you love the evening
She came to my chest and we fell into
the waterhole
                to which
since the grass had stopped singing and
was watching the sun sink
                I said
water is like love in tranquillity
my soul has wings of light and

never have I seen
   more beauty
than is in this evening
Her paw touched my lips as if
she loved me passionate and loud
so I said
                Loose lioness
and her lips took the words from my throat
her warm tongue flicking the living flutter
of my being
So I fumbled about in the darkness for my wings
and the grass looked all around at the evening

Libation

I have been throughout the world sleuthing,
drawing back goatheads
and from the writhing throats bloodletting,
watching the harassed religious eyes
whirl and freeze.

Earth drinks
the blood of fawns: jasmines
bloom in lions' eyes.

Breath and heat I have returned O Earth to your freedoms.
Now keep me virile and long at love:
let submission kiss off
the asking words from my lips.

Dying in a Mirthful Place

Dying in a mirthful place
I looked around at the dim lights
the hips and laughing throats
and the motions of the dance
and the wine the lovely wine

and turning to death said
  I thought you knew propriety
Death embarrassed stuttered
so I watched the lips
and hurried away to a hill in Arizona
where in the soil was such a noiseless
mirth and death
that I lay down and placed my head
  by a great boulder
The next morning I was dead
  excepting a few peripheral cells
and the buzzards
waiting for a savoring age to come
sat over me in mournful conversations
that sounded excellent to my eternal ear

When Rahman Rides

When Rahman rides a dead haste in a dusty wind
I wait for him and look for him coming over the desert
blustering through the tough unwaving leaves
and trembling behind a tall saguaro say
  O Rahman
and he says
          what what
  It's like this
          what what
so when I saw you coming I thought perhaps
There was the rush of dust and then farther on
a spiral whirlwinding
as if he had stopped too late and drawing up his wings
looked back at the saguaro's lifted arms
Unspiralling
he swept on across the desert
leaving me the ocotillo in a bloomless month

With Ropes of Hemp

With ropes of hemp
I lashed my body to the great oak
saying odes for the fiber of the oakbark
and the oakwood saying supplications
to the root mesh
deep and reticular in the full earth
through the night saying these
and early into the wild unusual dawn
chanting hysterical though quiet
watching the ropes ravel
and the body go raw
   while eternity
greater than the ravelings of a rope
waited with me patient in my experiment
Oh I said listening to the raucous
words of the nightclouds
how shadowy is the soul
how fleet with the wildness of wings

Under the grip of my bonds
I say Oh and melt beyond the ruthless coil
but return again saying odes in the night
where I stand splintered to the oak
gathering the dissentient ghosts of my spirit
into the oakheart
I in the night standing saying oaksongs
entertaining my soul to me

Doxology

I

Heterodoxy with Ennui

Should I bold in a moment intrude
upon a silence, hold my hands properly,
crossed, in a mock eternity,

would someone use my lips
for an expiation?

I have heard the silent owl near death
sees wildly with the comprehension of fire;
have drunk from those eyes.

Transplanted my soul to the wind, wound
my days round the algae of rapid streams,
wedded my bones to the throat of flame,
spirited.

You have heard it said of old time
the streets shall flow blood, but the streets
swept out with the flood
shall be deposited upon sand.
You have this word for a fulfillment.

An unconstrained fluidity prevails, abides;
whole notes are rocks
and men *thirty-second's,*
all in descending scales,
unvigiled bastardies of noise:
the motion of permanence.

Marble, pottery, signs endure,
support fluency, scrollwork,
where violins ornament, fingers,
offended with needles of care,
articulate poised domes.
This love for the thin and fleet
will race through the water-content
of my heavy death.

I die at the vernal equinox
and disorder like a kissing bug
quaffs my bonds: if I ascend,
I shall be congratulatory,
but if they fawn, desire
a season before immortality.

Detain me among the spiral designs
of an ancient amphora: fulfillment

comes before me like spiral designs
on an ancient amphora in which detain me,
fixed in rigid speed.

II

Orthodoxy with Achievement

Silent as light in dismal transit
through the void, I, evanescent,
sibilant among my parts,
fearing the eclipse of a possible glance
and not glancing, shut-eyed,
crouch froglike upon my brain,
hover and keep dark,
fervor opposed by dread,
activity numbed by its mixed result,
till some awaited drop falls
upon the mound and chaos
perfects the eternity of my silence.

I cannot count the forms,
thrown upon the wheel, delineated,
that have risen and returned
without accretion; but the spirit
drops falling upon wings
and preens the day with its call:
none say where in the silence it sleeps.

Though the sound of my voice
is a firmamental flaw, my self, in the rockheart,
in southern oakmoss blown tangled,
its supple pincers snaring
new forks of life, braiding thin limbs
of the wateroak on gooseberry hills
beside swamps where the raccoon runs
and dips his paw in the run-of-the-swamp
musky branchwater for darting crawfish
scuttling a mudwake before them; my self,
voluble in the dark side of hills
and placid bays, while the sun grows

increasing atmosphere to the sea,
correcting the fault of dawn; my self,
the drought of unforested plains,
the trilobite's voice,
the loquacity of an alien room troubled
by a blowfly, requires my entertainment
while we learn the vowels of silence.

III

Paradox with Variety

The temple stands in a rainforest
where bones have a quick ending.

Ephemeral as wings in fire
transparent leaves droop in the earth-steam;
growth and decay swallow the traces
of recent paths.

I went in. On one side sat the god of creation; on the other,
the god of destruction. Hatred held their eyes. Going deeper
to the next chamber, I found the god of destruction and the
god of creation tangled sensually on the floor; they gnawed
and procreated. In the next chamber was majesty: one god sat
staring at his golden walls.

I hear an organ playing through the morning rain;
it sounds like the memory of quilting women.
Between the organ and me, California poppies furl
like splotches of conceit
in the light and silent rain.
A robin peeks up from the grass
and rattles a ladybug in his beak.
Mr. Farnham says
life is fearfully complex.

When I was lustful I drew twenty maidens
from the Well of Sacrifice
and took them to Cozumel.
The priests of the steep temples

longed to smear my body
with blue ointment.
We've all died since
and all has been forgotten.
Strangers drop pebbles
into the Hole of Water:
it is too still.

Should I mistake khaki blood on foreign snow
for cherry ices, my mind would freeze;
but Red blood is interesting:
its vessels on the snow
are museums of eternity.

When stone and drought meet in high places,
the hand instructed by thirst
chips grace into solidity and Hellas,
like a broken grape upon marmoreal locks,
clarifies eternity. Had I come in the season
when sheep nibble windy grasses,
I would have gone out of the earth
listening for grasses
and the stippling feet of sheep
on sinking rocks.

I like to walk down windowless corridors
and going with the draft
feel the boost of perpendicularity,
directional and rigid;
concision of the seraphim,
artificial lighting.

Sometimes the price of my content
consumes its purchase
and martyrs' cries, echoing my peace,
rise sinuously like smoke
out of my ashen soul.

My Dice Are Crystal

My dice are crystal inlaid with gold
and possess
    spatial symmetry
about their centers and
mechanical symmetry and
    are of uniform density
and all surfaces have equal
coefficients of friction for

my dice are not loaded
    Thy will be done
whether dog or Aphrodite

Cleaning off a place on the ground
    I patted it
        flat and
        sat back on my legs
        rattling the bones
Apparitionally god sat poker-faced
silent on the other side
    When the ballooning
silence burst I cast
and coming to rest
the dice spoke their hard directive
    and melting
left gold bits on the soil

Having Been Interstellar

Having been interstellar
    and in the treble clef

by great expense of
    climbing mountains
    lighting crucible fires
in the catacombs

           among the hunted
      and the trapped in tiers
           seeking the distillate
           answering direct
      the draft of earthless air

      he turned in himself
           helplessly as in sleep

      and went out into the growth of rains
           and when the rains
                taking him
      had gone away in spring

           no one knew
      that he had ever flown
           he was no less
           no more known
      to stones he left a stone

Eolith

   I give you the wretched sympathy stone
   tears there is no end to the common matter
   dropped like suds water
      down garbage shutes in places
                     if you wish
   Enlil has whipped your thighs with cane
   and the possibility of unloading pity is
   not greater than my giving it
      there have been days like
                wasting
                     ziggurats while
   your past spoils what is quick like river flies
                days like
   the sweep of a steppe I have gone out
   like a northwind over the Nile
                          cavernous
   with Florida muddy hellish fountains of me it
   is quite terrible

to think of it
a shortening of days locusts dark west sounds
of oak limbs under pigeons
              splitting in the night
roof mounting troubling clay gods river wind
I have sketched pyramids for
              viewing splendid Hamlet
a task waking at night in dark speed
the pelican's over bays
   carrying this eolith

When I Set Fire to the Reed Patch

When I set fire to the reed patch
that autumn evening
the wind whipped volleys of shot
from the bursting joints
and armies bristling defensive interest
rushed up over the fringing hills
and stared into the fire

I laughed my self to death
and they
legs afire
eyelashes singed
swept in flooding up the lovely
expressions of popping light
and hissing thorns of flame

Clashing midfire
the armies quite unwound
the intentions of the fire
and snuffed the black reeds smoking out
but like destroyed mountains
left deposits
that will insure
deep mulch for next year's shoots
the greenest hope
autumn ever
left this patch of reeds

Coming to Sumer

Coming to Sumer and the tamarisks on the river
I Ezra with unsettling love
rifled the mud and wattle huts
for recent mournings
with gold leaves
and lapis lazuli beads
in the neat braids loosening from the skull
    Looking through the wattles to the sun
I said
It has rained some here in this place
unless snow falls heavily in the hills
to do this
    The floor was smooth with silt
and river weeds hanging gray
on the bent reeds spoke saying
Everything is even here as you can see
    Firing the huts
I abandoned the unprofitable poor
unequal even in the bone
    to disrespect
    and casual with certainty
watched an eagle wing as I went
to king and priest

I Struck a Diminished Seventh

I struck a diminished seventh
and sat down
to wait
    for the universal word
Come word
I said
azalea word
gel precipitate
while I
    the primitive spindle

binding the poles of earth and air
give you
with river ease
a superior appreciation
equalling winged belief
    It had almost come
I perishing for deity stood up
drying my feet
when the minor challenge was ignored
and death came over sieving me

In the Wind My Rescue Is

In the wind my rescue is
in whorls of it
    like winged tufts of dreams
bearing
   through the forms of nothingness
   the gyres and hurricane eyes
the seed safety
    of multiple origins

I set it my task
to gather the stones of earth
    into one place
the water modeled sand molded stones
   from
    the water images
    of riverbeds in drought
   from the boundaries of the mind
   from
    sloping farms
    and altitudes of ice and
to mount upon the highest stone
a cardinal
chilled in the attitude of song

But the wind has sown loose dreams
in my eyes

and telling unknown tongues
drawn me out beyond the land's end
and rising in long
parabolas of bliss
borne me safety
from all those ungathered stones

A Treeful of Cleavage Flared Branching

A treeful of cleavage flared branching
through my flesh and cagey
I sat down mid-desert
and heaping hugged up between my knees
an altarcone from the sand
and addressed it with water dreams

The wind
chantless of rain in the open place
spun a sifting hum
in slow circles round my sphere of grief
and the sun
inched countless arms
under the periphery of my disc of sight
eager for the golden thing

There must be time I said
to dream real these dreams
and the sun
startled by the sound of time
said Oh
and whirling in his arms
ran off across the sky
Heaping the sand
sharpening the cone of my god I said
I have oracles to seek

Drop leaf shade
the wet cuticle of the leaf tipped in shade
yielded belief

to the fixed will and there
where the wind like wisdom
sweeps clean the lust prints of the sun
lie my bones entombed
with the dull mound of my god
in bliss

I Assume the World Is Curious About Me

I assume the world is curious about me
                              the sound
                    and volume of hell
where brittle grace polished as glass
   glazed in fire glints
and pliant humility
furls coiling into itself
like an ashen abnegation
   for sin
you will want to see it
even without god is a hot consumption

I assume that when I die
going over and under without care
leaves will wilt and lose all windy interest
some ration of stars will fall
for my memorial

A simple thrust brings vomit
but a reduction
and retained separation has love in it
and love burns on itself
   while hate
is a cold expulsion and devastation

I assume many will crowd around me
to praise my unwillingness to simplify
then turning
assist in raising me to my outstanding tree
someday unhang my sinews from the nails
let down the gray locust from the pine

Gilgamesh Was Very Lascivious

Gilgamesh was very lascivious
and took the virgins as they ripened
from the men that wanted them
To the men Gilgamesh gave wall building
brick burning and gleaning of straw
for a physical expression
    yielding more protection
for the virgins the men wanted
than long hours in jogging beds
with the walls crumbling before
who knew what predators
    seeking wine
virgins
long fields of wheat
and spearshafts wrapped in gold

Because he sought the mate
    of his physical divinity
Gilgamesh
let many usurp the missing one
and went
singly in his tragic excellence

At his going by
the men in mud and sweat
saw virgins yielding to his eyes
    and turned to work with dreams
no virgin would ever give to them

Climbing the wall
and walking up and down upon it
I said
    Fools fools
but they kneaded slowly
the muscles of their glassy backs
    worms working in the sun

The Grass Miracles

The grass miracles have kept me down all autumn
purpose turning on me like an inward division
The grasses heading barbed tufts
airy panicles and purple spikes
have kept me stalled in the deadends
of branching dreams
    It is as though I had started up the trunk
and then dispersed like ant trails
along the branches
and out on the twigs
and paused dipping with a golden thought
at the points of the leaves

A black stump hidden
in grass and old melon vines
has reined my hurry
and I have gone up separately
    jiggling like a bubble flock
in globes of time

I have not been industrious this autumn
It has seemed necessary
to accomplish everything with a pause
    bending to part the grass
to what round fruit
becoming entangled in clusters
tying all the future up
in variations on present miracles

I Came in a Dark Woods Upon

I came in a dark woods upon
an ineffaceable difference
and oops embracing it
felt it up and down mindfully
    in the dark
prying open the knees to my ideas

It was slim and hard
with a sharp point
and stood up
its shaft shot deep as a pile

Who will extract I said desiring
a public value this erect
difference from the ground
    and the dryads
shifting in the limbs
dipped leaves
blotting the angels' roofeyes out

Taking the neck below the barbs
I eased the wet shaft up into my hands
    Everything retired
The dryads took body in the oakhearts
The angels shuttered their wintry peepholes
and flew off throneward across the fields
and the trees arms-up leaned as in wind away
and casting the difference
I splintered
    the whole environment

and somewhat dazed with grief ran
catching it up hot in my hands
and hurled it far into the seas
a brother to Excalibur

One Composing

One composing seminal works sat oblivious
by a brothel
and gave leaflets to the functions of the wind
saying
        Time is a liquid orb
where we swim loose
timeless in a total time
pursuing among the nuclear sediment

the sweet pale flakes of old events
    Stopping I watched the leaflets rock upward
from the windy alley
    and brought him a mug of stout
The contemporary he said
turning into the brothel
is an orb's shell
      of light
    within the liquid orb
and fertility came into him like a virtuoso
and mounting pubic realms
he rode galloping through the night
sweetsap and rain playing marbles
on the wind's speed of his outstretched shirt
      One
    weeping beads of ice
down the cold deserts of his brain
cried from the street O Jezebel
and the seminal one rose wiping saying
In exhaustion's death are dregs of wanted sleep

A Crippled Angel

A crippled angel bent in a scythe of grief
mourned in an empty lot
    Passing by I stopped
amused that immortality should grieve
and said
It must be exquisite

Smoke came out of the angel's ears
      the axles
    of slow handwheels of grief
and under the white lids of its eyes
bulged tears of purple light
Watching the agony diffuse in
      shapeless loss
I interposed a harp
    The atmosphere possessed it eagerly

and the angel
saying prayers for the things of time

let its fingers drop and burn
the lyric strings provoking wonder

Grief sounded like an ocean rose
        in bright clothes
and the fire
breaking out on the limbs rising
caught up the branching wings
    in a flurry of ascent
Taking a bow I shot transfixing
the angel midair
all miracle hanging fire
on rafters of the sky

Dropping Eyelids Among the Aerial Ash

Dropping eyelids among the aerial ash
I ascending entered the gates of cloud
westward where the sliver moon
        keeled in sun was setting
and sat down on a silver lining to think
my mind splintered with spears of glass
and errors of the cold
                    Below
the gorged god lay on the leveled city
and suburban bandaged
and drowsily tolled the reckonless waste
The clouds mushrooming rose
        and held about his head
like old incense of damp altars

Oh I said in the mistral of bleached
and naked thought
blood like a catalyst is evil's baptismal need
before the white rose and benefactions
rise

thin curls of hope from cooling lakes of ruin
and chiseled stone wins
    from the spout of human sacrifice
powers of mercy

Darkness pushed the sliver moon
from my silver lining and I arose
the high seed clouds fading
and went back down into the wounds and cries
and held up lanterns for the white nurses
moving quickly in the dark

I Came Upon a Plateau

I came upon a plateau
where mesquite roots
crazed the stone
   and rains
moved glinting dust
down the crevices
   Calling off rings
     to a council of peaks
I said
Spare me man's redundancy
and putting on bright clothes
sat down in the flat orthodoxy

Quivering with courtesy
a snake drew thrust in sines
and circles from his length
rearing coils of warning white
   Succumbing in the still ecstasy
sinuous through white rows of scales
I caved in upon eternity
saying this use is colorless

A pious person his heart
looted and burnt
   sat under a foundation

a windy cloak clutched round his bones
and said
When the razed temple cooled
I went in
and gathered these
relics of holy urns
Behold beneath this cloak
    and I looked in
at the dark whirls of dust

The peaks coughing bouldered
laughter shook to pieces
and the snake shed himself in ripples
across a lake of sand

Sumerian

I have grown a marsh dweller
subject to floods and high winds,
drinking brackish water on long hunts,
brushing gnat smoke
from clumps of reeds, have known

the vicissitudes of silt, of
shifting channels flush
by dark upland rains, of mounds
rising no more firmly than
monsters from the water:

on the southern salty
banks near the gulf the ducks
and flying vees of geese have
shunned me: the bouncing spider's net,
strung wet over narrows of reeds, has
broken terror dawn cold across my face:

rising with a handful of broken shells
from sifted underwater mud
I have come to know how high
the platform is, beyond approach,
of serenity and blue temple tiles.

Whose Timeless Reach

I Ezra the dying
portage of these deathless thoughts
stood on a hill in
the presence of the mountain
and said wisdom is
too wise for man it
is for gods and gods have little
use for it so I do not know what
to do with it
and animals use it only when
    their teeth start to fall and it
is too late to do anything
else but *be* wise and stay
out of the way
The eternal will not lie
down on any temporal hill
    The frozen mountain rose and broke
its tireless lecture of repose
and said death does
not take away it
ends giving halts bounty and
    Bounty I said thinking of ships
that I might take and helm right
out through space
dwarfing these safe harbors and
their values
taking the Way in whose timeless reach
cool thought unpunishable
by bones eternally glides

Driving Through

In the desert midnight I said
taking out my notebook I
    am astonished
though widely traveled having
seen Empire State and Palestine, Texas

and San Miguel de Allende
to mention extremes
and sharpened my pencil on the sole
    of my shoe

The mountains running skidded
over the icy mirages of the moon
and fell down tumbling
    laughing for breath
on the cool dunes
The stone mosaics of the flattest
places (parting lake-gifts) grouped
    in colors and
played games at imagery: a green
tiger with orange eyes, an Orpheus
with moving fingers
    Fontal the shrubs flooded
everything with cool
water

I sat down against a brimming smoketree
to watch and morning found the
desert reserved
trembling at its hot and rainless task
    Driving through
you would never suspect
the midnight rite or seeing my lonely house
guess it will someday hold
laurel and a friend

Song

Merging into place against a slope of trees,
I extended my arms and
took up the silence and spare leafage.
I lost my head first, the cervical meat
clumping off in rot,
baring the spinal heart to wind and ice

which work fast.

The environment lost no self-possession.
In spring, termites with tickling feet
aereated my veins.
A gall-nesting wren took my breath

flicking her wings, and
far into summer the termites found the heart.
No sign now shows the place,
all these seasons since,
but a hump of sod below the leaves
where chipmunks dig.

Choice

Idling through the mean space dozing,
blurred by indirection, I came upon a
stairwell and steadied a moment to
think against the stem:
upward turned golden steps
and downward dark steps entered the dark:

unused to other than even ground I
spurned the airless heights though bright
and the rigor to lift an immaterial soul
and sank
sliding in a smooth rail whirl and fell
asleep in the inundating dark
but waking said god abhors me
but went on down obeying at least
the universal law of gravity:

millenniums later waking in a lightened air
I shivered in high purity
and still descending grappled with
the god that
rolls up circles of our linear
sight in crippling disciplines
tighter than any climb.

Interval

Coming to a pinywoods
    where a stream darted across the path
like a squirrel or frightened blacksnake
I sat down on a sunny hillock
      and leaned back against a pine
and picked up some dry pineneedle bundles from the ground
and tore each bundle apart a needle at a time
    It was not Coulter's pine
    for *coulteri* is funnier looking
    and not Monterey either
and I thought God must have had Linnaeus in mind
orders of trees correspond so well between them
and I dropped to sleep wondering what design God
had meant the human mind to fit
      and looked up and saw a great bird
warming in the sun high on a pine limb
tearing from his breast golden feathers
    softer than new gold that
    dropped to the wind one or two
    gently and touched my face
I picked one up and it said
    The world is bright after rain
for rain washes death out of the land and hides it far
beneath the soil and it returns again cleansed with life
    and so all is a circle
and nothing is separable
Look at this noble pine from which you are
almost indistinguishable it is also sensible
    and cries out when it is felled
and so I said are trees blind and is the earth black to them
Oh if trees are blind
    I do not want to be a tree
A wind rising of *one in time* blowing the feather away
forsaken I woke
and the golden bird had flown away and the sun
had moved the shadows over me so I rose and walked on

This Black Rich Country

Dispossess me of belief:
between life and me obtrude
no symbolic forms:

grant me no mission: let my
mystical talents be beasts
in dark trees: thin the wire

I limp in space, melt it
with quick heat, let me walk
or fall alone: fail

me in all comforts:
hide renown behind the tomb:
withdraw beyond all reach of faith:

leave me this black rich country,
uncertainty, labor, fear: do not
steal the rewards of my mortality.

Look for My White Self

Find me diffuse, leached colorless,
gray as an inner image with no clothes
along the shallows of windrows: find

me wasted by hills,
conversion mountain blue in sight
offering its ritual cone of white:

over the plain I came long years,
drawn by gaze: a flat land with
some broken stems, no gullies,

sky matched square inch with
land in staying interchange: found

confusing hills, disconcerting names
and routes, differences locked
in seamless unities:

so look for my white self, age clear,
time cleaned: there is the mountain:
even now my blue

ghost may be
singing on that height of snow.

Apologia pro Vita Sua

I started picking up the stones
throwing them into one place
and by sunrise I was going far away
for the large ones
always turning to see never lost
the cairn's height
lengthening my radial reach:

the sun watched with deep concentration
and the heap through the hours grew
and became by nightfall
distinguishable from all the miles around
of slate and sand:

during the night the wind falling
turned earthward its lofty freedom and speed
and the sharp blistering sound muffled
toward dawn and the blanket was
drawn up over a breathless face:

even so you can see in full dawn
the ground there lifts
a foreign thing desertless in origin.

Hymn

I know if I find you I will have to leave the earth
and go on out
   over the sea marshes and the brant in bays
and over the hills of tall hickory
and over the crater lakes and canyons
and on up through the spheres of diminishing air
past the blackset noctilucent clouds
     where one wants to stop and look
way past all the light diffusions and bombardments
up farther than the loss of sight
   into the unseasonal undifferentiated empty stark

And I know if I find you I will have to stay with the earth
inspecting with thin tools and ground eyes
trusting the microvilli sporangia and simplest
   coelenterates
and praying for a nerve cell
with all the soul of my chemical reactions
and going right on down where the eye sees only traces

You are everywhere partial and entire
You are on the inside of everything and on the outside

I walk down the path down the hill where the sweetgum
has begun to ooze spring sap at the cut
and I see how the bark cracks and winds like no other bark
chasmal to my ant-soul running up and down
and if I find you I must go out deep into your
   far resolutions
and if I find you I must stay here with the separate leaves

Hymn II

   So when the year had come full round
   I rose
   and went out to the naked mountain

to see
the single peachflower on the sprout

blooming through a side of ribs
   possibly a colt's
and I endured each petal separately
and moved in orisons with the sepals

I lay
   said the sprouting stump
in the path of Liberty

Tyranny though I said is very terrible
and sat down leeward of the blossom
   to be blessed
and was startled by
a lost circling bee

The large sun setting red I went
down to the stream
   and wading in
let your cold water run over my feet

Hymn III

In the hour of extreme

   importance

when clots thicken
in outlying limbs and
   warmth retreats

to mourn
the thinning garrison of pulse

keep my tongue loose
to sing possible

   changes

that might redeem

might in iron phrases
    clang the skies

bells and my jangling eyes
ringing you in
    to claim me

shriven celebrant
your love's new-reasoned singer

   home

dead on arrival

Hymn IV

I hold you responsible for
every womb's neck
clogged with
killing growth

and for ducks on the bay
barking like hounds
all night
their wintering dreams

responsible for every action of
the brain that gives
me mind
and for all light

for the fishroe's
birth spawning forage to
night eels
nosing the tidal banks

I keep you existent at least as
a ghost crab

moon-extinguished his crisp
walk silenced on broken shells

answering at least as
the squiggling copepod
for the birthing and aging of
life's all-clustered grief

You have enriched us with
fear and contrariety
providing the searcher
confusion for his search

teaching by your snickering
wisdom an autonomy
for man
Bear it all

and keep me from my enemies'
wafered concision and zeal
I give you back to yourself
whole and undivided

Hymn V

Assure us you side with order: throw
off atomicities, dots, events, endless
successions: reveal an ancient inclination
we can adore and ritualize
with sapphirine cones and liturgies,
refine through ages of
canonical admissions and rejections; a
consistent, emerging inclination to prefer
the circling continuum, void receptacle,
and eternal now: spare

us the accidents, controversies, novelties,
constant adaptations, the working truths and
tentative assessments, the upheavals and unrest

of an unquiet past shaken by
the addition of a modern fact: package

knowledge, square-off questions, let them in
triumphs of finality be categorically
answered and filed: a
constant known yields all time to love: let our
words grow out of and strengthen the authority
of old rich usage, upholding what upholds.

The Watch

When the sun went down and the night came on
coming over the fields and up the driveway
to the rose arbor and the backporch posts

I gathered myself together from dispersing dark
and went up into the mountains
and sitting down on the round rock beyond the trees

kindled my thoughts
blowing the coals of my day's bright conscious
and said

all across the plains my voice going silently and down
among the stumps where the swamp cuts through
and in between among the villages of hill country

Now close your eyes
Sleep
Shut out the world from the dark sweet freshening
  of your quiet hearts
Lie loose in the deep waters
Do not be afraid to
give yourselves up to drowning in undefended rest

If a dust storm blows up out of the West I will run
down the mountain and go through all the homes

and wake you up

If a new fire appears in the sky I will let you know
in time
so you can know it should it claim you

I will have all your beings in mind burning like a watchfire
and when the night has grown thin and weak
and the full coyotes have given up their calls

I will move up close to the eternal and
saying nine praises
commend you to it and to the coming sun

March Song

At a bend in the stream by willows
I paused to be with the cattails
     their long flat leaves
and tall stems
bleached by wind and winter light

and winter had kept them
     edged down into the quiet eddy of the bend
tight with ice

O willows I said how you return
gold to the nakedness of your limbs
     coming again out of that country
into the longer sun

and Oh I said turning to the fluffy cattails
loosened to the approaching winds of spring
what a winter you leave in the pale stems
     of your becoming

Requiem

I

Mind

The strawberries along the roadbank in the hills bloomed,
the starwhite petals brilliant and melty in the sun as frost:
a glimmer of angels through the pines
    rained fine needles, blanketing the rich fruit.

On Rome's hills stand Respighi's musical pines,
aural columns of light, beingless but with minds.
Rising from banana trees in Mexico one, beyond
    the clouds, comes into skies of pines on rocky tops.

Thus when I saw the strawberries, I rose into the singing trees
and the angels, white
sharks in a glittering sea,
    massacred me.
My blood drops still to the red pulp of wild strawberries
whose white shark flowers
will call any man into the waters of the boughs.

Oh my mind runs down the moon's glass tears
and plucks them up (tektites) frozen from the land.

    No creation equals a moment's consciousness.
    No cymbal cones and crashes peaks so.
    No white shark stabs so.

Along the blade the dune thistle blows,
opening thorny hemispheres
of yellow florets half-deep in purple stain,
    and spears of onion grass rise sleek and clean
from the gray and gritty sand.
To stand with landward hair enduring these
requires sharks in the eyes, the backing of seas.

The coffin-carrier cries and the crow "cars" over the salt creeks.

2.

Event

The day after,
after the golden culminations and unfuneraled dead,
after the nuclear trees drifting
        on cloudy stems,
and the fruits of knowledge
and the knowledge of those golden high-capped trees,
        flaking, settling out,
after the transfigurations
and dark visitations,
        groans and twitching resentments,
after the golden culminations
and the trunks of violent trees stalking the vacant land,
        there rose an irrelevant dawn:

the white shell lay spiraled on the beach as it had lain
and the surf, again unheard,
        eased to primal rhythms
of jellyfishing heart, breaking into mind;
ants came out and withered in the sun;
        the white shark
sucked at the edge of the sea on the silent, scarlet morning;

and all the white souls sailing
sailed, funneling out into eternity;
        by the wharf, dolphin bobbled
belly-up with his poet, all his nudging sea-cleaning done;
briery the earth, iced
        with bones, rolled into time.

3.

Contraction

Repenting creation, God said,
        As you know, I Am,
God,
because I do not have to be consistent:
what was lawful to my general plan

       does not jibe
with my new specific will;
what the old law healed
is reopened
     in the new.
I have drawn up many covenants to eternity.

Returning silence unto silence,
the Sumerian between the rivers lies.
His skull crushed and moded into rock
     does not leak or peel.
The gold earring lies in the powder
of his silken, perished lobe.
The incantations, sheep trades, and night-gatherings
     with central leaping fires,
roar and glare still in the crow's-foot
walking of his stylus on clay.
Under surgery the sick man rolls and
     vomits on the temple floor,
the anesthetic words of reciting priests
licking grooves through his frantic mind.
The dust has dried up all his tears.
     He sleeps out the old unending drug of time.

The rose dies, man dies, the world dies, the god
grows and fails, the born universe dies
     into renewal,
and all endures the change,
totally lost and totally retained.

Ritual for Eating the World

     At a bend in the rocks there hung
     inexplicably a rope
     and musing I said
     When I die don't bury me
     under no weeping willer tree

     It's I thought a hangman's loop

provided by my warmer ghoul to
raise me out of care

or god's own private fishing hook
for glaring people
who sit wasted in the sun
on rocks

But put me up in a high dry place
unavailable to the coyote's face

It's what I said old mountain
climbers left
dangling

The wind rides blade on mesa tops

Oh when I die don't bury me
under no weeping willer tree

and there being besides old bush
and distance nothing but a rope
I engaged myself with it but

it broke
and all through the heaving night
making day I faced

piecemeal the sordid
reacceptance of my world

The Wide Land

Having split up the chaparral
blasting my sight
the wind said
    You know I'm
        the result of
forces beyond my control
I don't hold it against you

I said
It's all right I understand

Those pressure bowls and cones
the wind said
are giants in their continental gaits
I know I said I know
they're blind giants
Actually the wind said I'm
   if anything beneficial
     resolving extremes
filling up lows with highs
No I said you don't have
to explain
It's just the way things are

Blind in the wide land I
turned and risked my feet
to loose stones and sudden

alterations of height

Spring Song

I picked myself up from the dust again
and went on
phoenix not with another set of wings but with
no other choice
Oh I said to my soul may a deep
luminosity seize you
and my blanched soul smiled from its need and
dwelt on in the pale country of its bones

A field opened on the right
and I went in
slipping arms-high through bleaches
of golden broom grass
and whirled with the wind sizzling there

Look said the golden tussocks and I
looked down at the rising shoots

Where, if spring will not keep you,
will you go
I said to the broom straws
so I cried
and stooping to scold the shoots fell
in with their green enhancing tips
and nearly died
getting away from the dividing place

At dusk the sun set and it was dark and having
found no place to leave my loyalty
I slaughtered it by the road and spilled its
blood on sand while the red moon rose

Batsto

After two gray sunless days of warm
noreaster windy rains the sun breaking
clear this morning, over the bayside
field the sparrowhawk foraging in the
oval air, we took Route 9 north through
Pleasantville, past the pleasant
inviting cemetery crisp with light,
over the railroad, crosstown to the
Absecon meadows and into the sycamore
leaf-letting hills beyond and through
the housing development with groves
of old leaf-keeping darker oaks and

northward past Seaview Country Club
with the high round dining room and
young rich men in casuals crossing the
street to the golf-links and on past
fields and hedges, the scarlotry of
maple leaves, sassafras and skinny
birch resplendent in the clean sun,
the winding flat highway, empty
but for slight local traffic, and onto
Garden State Parkway to bridge the

wide-mouthed Mullica River that spreads
out in brown still meadows to the sea,
an occasional gull, the skeletal
cedar upriver against the land, off
to secondary roads not too well marked
and along the north bank of the
Mullica westward into the Wharton
Tract, now a state park, with ghost
towns and endless acres in neglect,

stopping at a pinerise to see the
cemetery of the French family, death
after more than a century light as
the morning sun, where Thomas French,
a year older than his wife, lies since
1844, his wife three years later
giving up her heavy grief, lying
down beside him, their secret union
invisible in the green needles of
the great pine that branches now
into their rest, looking where Levi
Scott, four years old in 1800, went
down beneath his thin tall slab, may
the child keep innocent of treason, and

on to Crowley Landing on the left
between river and road, now a campsite
and picnic ground, where we took
pictures, wild mullein starring the
grounds, a yucca group with dead
flower-spears off in a clearing, in
the center a mound of old chimney
bricks with wasp dust and gold grasses
and a yard tree, broken off, with
slender sprouts nude, swamp cedar
standing around in clumps like persons
edging the openings, by the river now
narrower twists of white birch
thin-twigged and leafless, and

around two curves to Batsto, the
tower of the mansion house first seen,

like the towers of shore women gazing
the sea's return, a confluence of
roads and streams, the bog-iron works
and Revolutionary cannon balls, iron
hearths and iron oxen-shoes, seeing
a nail made and headed from nail rod,
the company store, and men from
Trenton writing the place up for the
Sunday paper, wasps drunk with fall
warmth, a beautiful November noon by
the grist mill and the meal-honed
wood, the carriage house and small
seats, the sty with the iron-bowled
furnace for scalding, on the third
floor of the mansion a strict stairway
to the slaves' underground railroad,
and

weakening to the presence of a foreign
past and to the keeping of old things,
back home by Route 30 and the White
Horse Pike, by the farmers' stands,
Naval Air Base and to the sea's edge.

Come Prima

I know
there is
perfection in the being
of my being,
that I am
holy in amness
as stars or
paperclips,

that the universe,
moving from void to void,

pours in and out
through me:

there is a point,
only itself,
that fills space,
an emptiness
that is plenitude:

a void that is all being,
a being that is void:

I am perfect:
the wind is perfect:
ditchwater, running, is perfect:
everything is:

I raise my hand

Composing

An orchestration of events,
memories,
intellections, of the wounds,
hard throats, the perils
of the youthful private member:
a clustering of years into phrases,
motifs, a

keying to somber D-flat
or brilliant A:
an emergence
of minor meanings,
the rising of flutes, oboes, bassoons:
percussion,
the critical cymbal

crashing grief out
or like a quivering fan unfolding

into spirit:
the derelict breakage of days, weeks,
hours, re-organizing,
orienting
to the riding movement,

hawklike,
but keener in wings,
in shadow deeper:
a swerving into the underside
gathering
dream-images,
the hidden coursing of red-black cries,

darkness,
the ghosts re-rising,
the eyeless, crippled, furious,
mangled ones:
then two motions like cliffs
opposing, the orchestration at
first

too torn, but going back
finding new lights to doom
the dark resurrections
until the large curve of meaning
stands apart
like a moon-cusp or horn
singing with a higher soundless sound.

Mountain Liar

The mountains said they were
        tired of lying down
and wanted to know what
        I could do about
getting them off the ground

Well close your eyes I said
        and I'll see if I can

by seeing into your nature
    tell where you've been wronged
What do you think you want to do
    They said Oh fly

My hands are old
    and crippled keep no lyre
but if that is your true desire
    and conforms roughly
with your nature I said
    I don't see why
we shouldn't try
    to see something along that line

Hurry they said and snapped shut
    with rocky sounds their eyes
I closed mine and sure enough
    the whole range flew
gliding on interstellar ice

They shrieked with joy and peeked
    as if to see below
but saw me as before there
    foolish without my lyre
We haven't budged they said
    You wood

Gravelly Run

I don't know somehow it seems sufficient
to see and hear whatever coming and going is,
losing the self to the victory
    of stones and trees,
of bending sandpit lakes, crescent
round groves of dwarf pine:

for it is not so much to know the self
as to know it as it is known
    by galaxy and cedar cone,

as if birth had never found it
and death could never end it:

the swamp's slow water comes
down Gravelly Run fanning the long
    stone-held algal
hair and narrowing roils between
the shoulders of the highway bridge:

holly grows on the banks in the woods there,
and the cedars' gothic-clustered
    spires could make
green religion in winter bones:

so I look and reflect, but the air's glass
jail seals each thing in its entity:

no use to make any philosophies here:
    I see no
god in the holly, hear no song from
the snowbroken weeds: Hegel is not the winter
yellow in the pines: the sunlight has never
heard of trees: surrendered self among
    unwelcoming forms: stranger,
hoist your burdens, get on down the road.

Prospecting

Coming to cottonwoods, an
orange rockshelf,
and in the gully
an edging of stream willows,

I made camp
and turned my mule loose
to graze in the dark
evening of the mountain.

Drowsed over the coals
and my loneliness

like an inner image went
out and shook
hands with the willows,

and running up the black scarp
tugged the heavy moon
up and over into light,

and on a hill-thorn of sage
called with the coyotes
and told ghost stories to
a night circle of lizards.
Tipping on its handle
the Dipper unobtrusively
poured out the night.

At dawn returning, wet
to the hips with meetings,
my loneliness woke me up
and we merged refreshed into
the breaking of camp and day.

Jersey Cedars

The wind inclines the cedars and lets
snow riding in
bow them
        swaying weepers
           on the hedgerows of
           open fields

black-green branches stubby fans under snow
bent spires dipping at the ground

Oh said the cedars will spring let us rise
and I said rain
will thawing
        unburden you
         and will

they said
we stand again green-cone arrows at the sun
The forces I said are already set up

but they splintering in that deep soft day
could not herd
their moans
                    into my quiet speech
                    and I bent
                    over arms

dangling loose to wind and snow to be
with them assailing the earth with moans

Joshua Tree

            The wind
        rounding the gap
    found me there
        weeping under a
                Joshua tree
        and Oh I said
    I am mortal all right
        and cannot live,
                by roads
        stopping to wait
    for no one coming,
        moving on
                to dust
        and burned weeds,
    having no liturgy,
        no pilgrim
                from my throat
        singing wet news of joy,
    no dome, alabaster wall,
        no eternal city:
                the wind said
        Wayfaring and wandering

is not for mortals
  who should raise
      the cock
  that cries their
dawns in and
  cannot always be coming to´un-
      broken country:
  settle here
by this Joshua tree
  and make a well:
      unlike wind
  that dies and
never dies I said
  I must go on
      consigned to
  form that will not
let me loose
  except to death
      till some
  syllable's rain
anoints my tongue
  and makes it sing
      to strangers:
  if it does not rain
find me wasted by roads:
  enter angling through
      my cage
  and let my ribs
sing me out.

A Symmetry of Thought

is a mental object:
is to spirit
a rock of individual shape,
a flowerbed, pylon,
an arbor vitae
to cerebral loam:
is a moon in the mind,

water and land divided,
a crystal, precipitate,
separation, refinement,
a victory of being over void,
hazardous commitment,
broken eternity,
limited virtue;
coming into matter
spirit fallen
trades eternity
for temporal form:
is a symmetry of motion,
can always find its way
back to oblivion,
must move accommodating,
useful, relevant:
is, dead, a perfection;
here is its cage
to contemplate; here
time stops
and all its hollow bells
struck loud are
silenced in the never-ending sound.

Thaw

Winter over, ice-bound
mind better not
rush to a spring-meet fast;
might trip, stiff thoughts,
        shatter:
better not warm up too
close to sun;
might melt, run, gullies
caking off the good
firm country of the brain.

Better go slow,
bend with the gradual movement,

let sap flow but
keep an eye on any
thermal swell rising at
   glassy mind.

If it gets loose wind
will take it
riddling through the underbrush,
but if it stays
solid brilliant ice
tulip root
   warm in coming
will splinter it.

The Wind Coming Down From

   summit and blue air
said I am sorry for you
and lifting past
   said you
are mere dust which I
   as you see control

yet nevertheless are
   instrument of miracle

and rose
   out of earshot but
returning in a slow loop
   said while
I am always just this bunch of
   compensating laws
pushed, pushing
   not air or motion
but the motion of air

I coughed
   and the wind said
Ezra will live

to see your last
    sun come up again

I turned (as I will) to weeds and
the wind went off
    carving
monuments through a field of stone
    monuments whose shape
wind cannot arrest but
taking hold on
    changes

while Ezra
    listens from terraces of mind
wind cannot reach or
weedroots of my low-feeding shiver

Return

I

drought continuing
the stems
drop their leaves

healing hard the pulvinal
scars and
dangling buzzards

drop to sleeps
in ledge and
cactus shade, to rockheld

reservoirs of night
and
sidewinder from the

stinging air
holds
his tongue

2

I have come a long way
without arriving
torn songs up

from the roots of weeds
but made no
silence sing:

climbed the peak but
found no foothold
higher than the ground

3

should I roll
rocks
down the slope

to learn
the thunder of
my being:

should I call out,
echolocation fixing me
against a certain wall:

should I break
a switch
and whirling inscribe

a circle round me
to know my
center and periphery

4

the leaves drop:
wolves thinning
like moons run through scuds of sage:

moon cloud shadows
sail gulfs
through a wild terrain

Silver

I thought Silver must have snaked logs
       when young:
she couldn't stand to have the line brush her lower hind leg:
in blinded halter she couldn't tell what had loosened behind her
              and was coming
as downhill
to rush into her crippling her to the ground:

and when she almost went to sleep, me dreaming at the slow plow,
I would
at dream's end turning over the mind to a new chapter
          let the line drop and touch her leg
          and she would
bring the plow out of the ground with speed but wisely
fall soon again into the slow requirements of our dreams:
how we turned at the ends of rows without sense to new furrows
and went back
          flicked by
          cornblades and hearing the circling in
the cornblades of horseflies in pursuit:

I hitch up early, the raw spot on Silver's shoulder
sore to the collar,
get a wrench and change the plow's bull-tongue for a sweep,
and go out, wrench in my hip pocket for later adjustments,
          down the ditch-path
by the white-bloomed briars, wet crabgrass, cattails,
              and rusting ferns,
riding the plow handles down,
   keeping the sweep's point from the ground,
the smooth bar under the plow gliding,
the traces loose, the raw spot wearing its soreness out
in the gentle movement to the fields:

          when snake-bitten in the spring pasture grass
Silver came up to the gate and stood head-down enchanted
              in her fate
I found her sorrowful eyes by accident and knew:

nevertheless the doctor could not keep her from all
the consequences, rolls in the sand, the blank extension
          of limbs,
          head thrown back in the dust,
useless unfocusing eyes, belly swollen
wide as I was tall
and I went out in the night and saw her in the solitude
          of her wildness:

but she lived and one day half got up
and looking round at the sober world took me back
          into her eyes
and then got up and walked and plowed again;
mornings her swollen snake-bitten leg wept bright as dew
and dried to streaks of salt leaked white from the hair.

Mule Song

Silver will lie where she lies
sun-out, whatever turning the world does,
longeared in her ashen, earless,
floating world:
indifferent to sores and greenage colic,
where oats need not
come to,
bleached by crystals of her trembling time:
beyond all brunt of seasons, blind
forever to all blinds,
inhabited by
brooks still she may wraith over broken
fields after winter
or roll in the rye-green fields:
old mule, no defense but a mule's against
disease, large-ribbed,
flat-toothed, sold to a stranger, shot by a
stranger's hand,
not my hand she nuzzled the seasoning-salt from.

Hardweed Path Going

   Every evening, down into the hardweed
going,
the slop bucket heavy, held-out, wire handle
freezing in the hand, put it down a minute, the jerky
smooth unspilling levelness of the knees,
    meditation of a bucket rim,
lest the wheat meal,
floating on clear greasewater, spill,
down the grown-up path:

    don't forget to slop the hogs,
    feed the chickens,
    water the mule,
    cut the kindling,
    build the fire,
    call up the cow:

    supper is over, it's starting to get
dark early,
better get the scraps together, mix a little meal in,
nothing but swill.

   The dead-purple woods hover on the west.
I know those woods.
Under the tall, ceiling-solid pines, beyond the edge of
field and brush, where the wild myrtle grows,
   I let my jo-reet loose.
A jo-reet is a bird. Nine weeks of summer he
sat on the well bench in a screened box,
a stick inside to walk on,
    "jo-reet," he said, "jo-reet."
    and I
would come up to the well and draw the bucket down
deep into the cold place where red and white marbled
clay oozed the purest water, water celebrated
throughout the county:
    "Grits all gone?"
    "jo-reet."

Throw a dipper of cold water on him. Reddish-black
flutter.
> "reet, reet, reet!"

> Better turn him loose before
cold weather comes on.
>> Doom caving in
>> inside
>> any pleasure, pure
>> attachment
>> of love.

Beyond the wild myrtle away from cats I turned him loose
and his eye asked me what to do, where to go;
he hopped around, scratched a little, but looked up at me.
Don't look at me. Winter is coming.
Disappear in the bushes. I'm tired of you and will
be alone hereafter. I will go dry in my well.
> I will turn still.
Go south. Grits is not available in any natural form.
Look under leaves, try mushy logs, the floors of pinywoods.
South into the dominion of bugs.

> They're good woods.
But lay me out if a mourning dove far off in the dusky pines
> starts.

> Down the hardweed path going,
leaning, balancing, away from the bucket, to
Sparkle, my favorite hog, sparse, fine black hair,
grunted while feeding if rubbed,
scratched against the hair, or if talked to gently:
got the bottom of the slop bucket:
>> "Sparkle . . .
>> You hungry?
>> Hungry, girly?"
blowing, bubbling in the trough.

> Waiting for the first freeze:

"Think it's going to freeze tonight?" say the neighbors,
the neighbors, going by.

       Hog-killing.

Oh, Sparkle, when the axe tomorrow morning falls
and the rush is made to open your throat,
I will sing, watching dry-eyed as a man, sing my
       love for you in the tender feedings.

       She's nothing but a hog, boy.

Bleed out, Sparkle, the moon-chilled bleaches
       of your body hanging upside-down
hardening through the mind and night of the first freeze.

Terminus

Coming to a rockwall
I looked back
to the winding gulch
and said
is this as far as you can go:

and the gulch, rubble
frazzled with the windy remains
of speech, said
comers here turn and go back:

so I sat down, resolved
to try
the problem out, and
every leaf fell
from my bush of bones

and sand blew down the winding
gulch and
eddying

rounded out a bowl
from the terminal wall:

I sat in my bones' fragile shade
and worked the
knuckles of my mind till
the altering earth broke to
mend the fault:

I rose and went through.

Close-Up

Are all these stones
        yours
I said
and the mountain
pleased

but reluctant to
admit my praise could move it much

shook a little
and rained a windrow ring of stones
to show
that it was so

Stonefelled I got
up addled with dust

and shook
        myself
without much consequence

Obviously I said it doesn't pay
to get too

close up to
          greatness

and the mountain friendless wept
          and said
it couldn't help
itself

Grassy Sound

It occurred to me there are no
     sharp corners
          in the wind
and I was very glad to think
     I had so close
          a neighbor
to my thoughts but decided to
     sleep before
          inquiring

The next morning I got up early
     and after yesterday had come
          clear again went
down to the salt marshes
     to talk with
          the straight wind there
I have observed I said
     your formlessness
          and am

enchanted to know how
     you manage loose to be
          so influential

The wind came as grassy sound
     and between its
          grassy teeth
spoke words said with grass
     and read itself

on tidal creeks as on
the screens of oscilloscopes
   A heron opposing
    it rose wing to wind

turned and glided to another creek
   so I named a body of water
    Grassy Sound
and came home dissatisfied there
   had been no
    direct reply
but rubbed with my soul an
   apple to eat
    till it shone

Bourn

When I got past relevance
the singing shores
told me to turn back

but I took the outward gray
to be
some meaning of foreign light

trying to get through and
when I looked back I saw
the shores were dancing

willows of grief and
from willows it was not far to
look back on waves

So I came to
the decimal of being,
entered and was gone

What light there

72   *A. R. Ammons · Collected Poems*

no tongue turns to tell
to willow and calling shore

though willows weep and shores sing always

Orientale

The pebble spoke and down
came the sun
    its plume
brushing through space as

over smooth sea-reaching stream
bent reed
    lets sodden leaf
arrow-ripples cut

and acorn husk wind-whirled
ran out and caught the sun
    in its burred cup
and said Look

to everyone standing on
edge of fern leaf watching
    the other edge
become imaginary as

waterbirds low-flying through
islands snake-long dark offshore
    Acorn husk got
no attention and even

the universe could sundering
hold no ear
    What somebody asked did
the pebble say

and sea colander washed
aland said Nothing

nothing exists
and everybody watched to

see if fern leaf could
re-appear with its lost edge
    and when
snow fell went in

Possibility Along a Line of Difference

At the crustal
discontinuity
I went down and
walked
on the gravel bottom,
head below gully rims

tufted with
clumpgrass and
through-free roots:
prairie flatness crazed
by that difference,
I grew

excited with
the stream's image left
in dust
and farther down
in confined rambling
I

found a puddle
green, iridescent
with a visitation of daub-singing wasps,
sat down and watched
tilted shadow untilting
fill the trough,

imagined cloudbursts
and

scattered pillars of rain,
buffalo at night routed
by lightning,
leaping,

falling back,
wobble-kneed calves
tumbling, gully-caught;
coyote, crisp-footed
on the gravel,
loping up the difference.

Back Country

The sun binds:
the small cold
moon
leading spins you,
    marionette:
the silver ruts of backwoods roads
narrowing
straiten your interests:

    you keep moving:
return is to your vitiations:
ahead, the road,
pure of you;
    the pasture hills
fractured with
hurls
of white rock,

    unsurrendered to
your spoiling eyes;
plum blossoms
uncast at your breath:
    you have come
to back country:

hogweed's hard yellow
heads

   crowd the ruts
apart: there are
wagon tracks
and, splitting the weed,
   the hoofprints
of long-stepping, unshod mules:
the hill people will
not discern

   your wound:
you will pitch hay,
wash your
face in a staved bucket,
   soap your arms with
chinaberry leaves,
rinse
well-water clean:

   no: they will know
you:
keep on:
the sun calls:
   the moon has you:
the ruts
diminish you to distance:
a hill puts you out.

Mansion

So it came time
   for me to cede myself
and I chose
the wind
   to be delivered to

The wind was glad
   and said it needed all

the body
it could get
        to show its motions with

and wanted to know
        willingly as I hoped it would
if it could do
something in return
        to show its gratitude

When the tree of my bones
        rises from the skin I said
come and whirlwinding
stroll my dust
        around the plain

so I can see
        how the ocotillo does
and how saguaro-wren is
and when you fall
        with evening

fall with me here
        where we can watch
the closing up of day
and think how morning breaks

Prodigal

After the shifts and dis-
continuities, after the congregations of orders,
    black masses floating through
    mind's boreal clarity, icebergs in fog,
flotillas of wintering ducks weathering the night,
    chains of orders, multifilamentous chains
    knobbed with possibility, disoriented
chains, winding back on themselves, unwinding,
    intervolving, spinning, breaking off

    (nomads clustering at dusk into tents of sleep,

disorganizing, widening out again with morning)
    after the mental

    blaze and gleam,
the mind in both motions building and tearing down,
    running to link effective chains,
    establish molecules of meaning,
frameworks, to
    perfect modes of structuring
    (so days can bend to trellising
and pruned take shape,
    bloom into necessary event)

    after these motions, these vectors,
orders moving in and out of orders, collisions
    of orders, dispersions, the grasp weakens,

    the mind whirls, short of the unifying
reach, short of the heat
    to carry that forging:
    after the visions of these losses, the spent
seer, delivered to wastage, risen
    into ribs, consigns knowledge to
    approximation, order to the vehicle
of change, and fumbles blind in blunt innocence
    toward divine, terrible love.

Mechanism

Honor a going thing, goldfinch, corporation, tree,
    morality: any working order,
    animate or inanimate: it

has managed directed balance,
    the incoming and outgoing energies are working right,
    some energy left to the mechanism,

some ash, enough energy held

to maintain the order in repair,
assure further consumption of entropy,

expending energy to strengthen order:
        honor the persisting reactor,
        the container of change, the moderator: the yellow

bird flashes black wing-bars
        in the new-leaving wild cherry bushes by the bay,
        startles the hawk with beauty,

flitting to a branch where
        flash vanishes into stillness,
        hawk addled by the sudden loss of sight:

honor the chemistries, platelets, hemoglobin kinetics,
        the light-sensitive iris, the enzymic intricacies
        of control,

the gastric transformations, seed
        dissolved to acrid liquors, synthesized into
        chirp, vitreous humor, knowledge,

blood compulsion, instinct: honor the
        unique genes,
        molecules that reproduce themselves, divide into

sets, the nucleic grain transmitted
        in slow change through ages of rising and falling form,
        some cells set aside for the special work, mind

or perception rising into orders of courtship,
        territorial rights, mind rising
        from the physical chemistries

to guarantee that genes will be exchanged, male
        and female met, the satisfactions cloaking a deeper
        racial satisfaction:

heat kept by a feathered skin:
        the living alembic, body heat maintained (bunsen

burner under the flask)

so the chemistries can proceed, reaction rates
       interdependent, self-adjusting, with optimum
       efficiency—the vessel firm, the flame

staying: isolated, contained reactions! the precise and
       necessary worked out of random, reproducible,
       the handiwork redeemed from chance, while the

goldfinch, unconscious of the billion operations
       that stay its form, flashes, chirping (not a
       great songster) in the bay cherry bushes wild of leaf.

Guide

      You cannot come to unity and remain material:
in that perception is no perceiver:
    when you arrive
you have gone too far:
      at the Source you are in the mouth of Death:

you cannot
    turn around in
the Absolute: there are no entrances or exits
      no precipitations of forms
to use like tongs against the formless:
    no freedom to choose:

to be
      you have to stop not-being and break
off from *is* to *flowing* and
    this is the sin you weep and praise:
origin is your original sin:
      the return you long for will ease your guilt
and you will have your longing:

    the wind that is my guide said this: it
should know having

       given up everything to eternal being but
direction:

how I said can I be glad and sad: but a man goes
   from one foot to the other:
wisdom wisdom:
      to be glad and sad at once is also unity
and death:
   wisdom wisdom: a peachblossom blooms on a particular
tree on a particular day:
      unity cannot do anything in particular:

are these the thoughts you want me to think I said but
   the wind was gone and there was no more knowledge then.

The Golden Mean

        What does
wisdom say:
   wisdom says
     do not put too much stress
on doing; sit some and wait,
   if you can get
     that self-contained:
but do not sit too much;
   being can wear thin
     without experience:
not too much stress on thrift
   at the expense of living;
     immaterial things like
life must be conserved against
   materiality: however,
     spending every dime you make
can exhaust all boundaries,
   destroy resources and
     recovery's means:
not too much stress on knowledge;
   understanding, too, is a
     high faculty
that should bear pleasurably on facts;

ordering, aligning,
    comparing,
as processes, become diffuse in too
    much massiveness:
        but the acquisition
of thinking stuff is crucial
    to knowledge
        and to understanding:
wisdom says
    do not love exceedingly:
        you must withhold
enough to weather loss;
    however, love thoroughly
        and with the body
so women will respect and fear the little
    man: though dainty
        they will scoff
when not profoundly had: not too much
    mind over body or
        body over mind;
they are united in this life and should
    blend to dual good or ill:
        and do not stress
wisdom too much: if you lean neither
    way, the golden
        mean narrows
and rather than a way becomes a wire,
    or altogether
        vanishes, a
hypothetical line from which extremes
    perpendicularly begin:
        and if you do not
violate wisdom to some extent,
    committing yourself fully,
        without reserve,
and foolishly, you will not become *one*,
    capable of direction,
        selected to a single aim,
and you will be notable for nothing:
    nothing in excess is
        excessive nothingness:
go: but wisdom says do not go too far.

Risks and Possibilities

Here are some pretty things picked for you:

    1)   dry thunder
            rustling like water
            down the sky's eaves

            is summer locust
            in dogfennel weed

    2)   the fieldwild
            yellow daisy
               focusing dawn

            inaugurates
            the cosmos

    3)   the universe comes
               to bear
            on a willow-slip and
            you cannot unwind
               a pebble
            from its constellations

    4)   chill frog-gibber
            from grass
               or loose stone
            is

            crucial as fieldwild
            yellow daisy:

such propositions:
each thing boundless in its effect,
   eternal in the working out
of its effect: each brush
of beetle-bristle against a twig
   and the whole
shifts, compensates, realigns:
the crawl of a slug

    on the sea's floor
quivers the moon to a new dimension:
bright philosophy,
    shake us all! here on the
bottom of an ocean of space
we babble words recorded
    in waves
of sound that
cannot fully disappear,
    washing up
like fossils on the shores of unknown worlds:

    nevertheless, taking our identities,
    we accept destruction:

    a tree, committed as a tree,
    cannot in a flood
       turn fish,
    sprout gills (leaves are
       a tree's gills) and fins:
       the molluscs
    dug out of mountain peaks
    are all dead:

oh I will be addled and easy and move
over this prairie in the wind's keep,
long-lying sierras blue-low in the distance:
I will glide and say little
(what would you have me say? I know nothing;
still, I cannot help singing)
and after much grace
I will pause
and break cactus water to your lips:

identity's strict confinement! a risk
    and possibility,
granted by mercy:
in your death is the mercy of your granted life:
    do not quibble:

    dry thunder in the locust weed!
    the supple willow-slip leafless in winter!

the chill gibber of the frog
stilled in nightsnake's foraging thrust!
how ridiculous!
grim:
  enchanting:

repeating mid night these songs for these divisions.

Bridge

A tea garden shows you how:

you sit in rhododendron shade
at table
on a pavilion-like lawn

the sun midafternoon through the blooms
and you

watch lovers and single people
go over the steep moonbridge at the pond's narrows

where flies nip circles

in the glass
and vanish in the widening sight except for an uncertain

gauze memory of wings

and as you sip from the small thick cup
held bird-warm
in the hands

you watch
the people
rising on the bridge

descend into the pond,

where bridge and mirrorbridge merge

at the bank
returning their images to themselves:
a grove
of pepper trees (sgraffito)
screens them into isolations of love or loneliness:

it is enough from this to think in the green tea scent
and turn to farther things:

when the spirit comes to the bridge of consciousness
and climbs higher and higher
toward the peak no one reaches live
but where ascension
and descension meet
completing the idea of a bridge

think where the body is,
that going too deep

it may lose touch,
wander a ghost in hell
sing irretrievably in gloom,
and think

how the spirit silvery with vision may
break loose in high wind

and go off weightless

body never to rise or spirit fall again to unity,
to lovers strolling through pepper-tree shade:

paradise was when
Dante
regathered from height and depth
came out onto the soft, green, level earth

into the natural light, come, sweat, bloodblessings,
and thinning sheaf of days.

The Foot-Washing

Now you have come,
the roads
humbling your feet with dust:

I ask you to
sit by this
spring:

I will wash your feet
with springwater
and silver care:

I lift leaking handbowls
to your ankles:
O ablutions!

Who are you
sir
who are my brother?

I dry your feet
with sweetgum
and mint leaves:

the odor of your feet
is newly earthen,
honeysuckled:

bloodwork in blue
raisures over the white
skinny anklebone:

if I have wronged you
cleanse me with the falling
water of forgiveness.

And woman, your flat feet
yellow, gray with dust,

your orphaned udders flat,

lift your dress
up to your knees
and I will wash your feet:

feel the serenity
cool as cool springwater
and hard to find:

if I have failed to know
the grief in your gone time,
forgive me wakened now.

Coon Song

I got one good look
        in the raccoon's eyes
                when he fell from the tree
came to his feet
        and perfectly still
                seized the baying hounds
in his dull fierce stare,
        in that recognition all
                decision lost,
choice irrelevant, before the
        battle fell
                and the unwinding
of his little knot of time began:

                Dostoevsky would think
it important if the coon
        could choose to
                be back up the tree:
or if he could choose to be
        wagging by a swamp pond,
                dabbling at scuttling
crawdads: the coon may have
        dreamed in fact of curling

into the holed-out gall
of a fallen oak some squirrel
had once brought
high into the air
clean leaves to: but

reality can go to hell
is what the coon's eyes said to me:
and said how simple
the solution to my
problem is: it needs only
not to be: I thought the raccoon
felt no anger,
saw none; cared nothing for cowardice,
bravery; was in fact
bored at
knowing what would ensue:
the unwinding, the whirling growls,
exposed tenders,
the wet teeth—a problem to be
solved, the taut-coiled vigor
of the hunt
ready to snap loose:

you want to know what happened,
you want to hear me describe it,
to placate the hound's-mouth
slobbering in your own heart:
I will not tell you: actually the coon
possessing secret knowledge
pawed dust on the dogs
and they disappeared, yapping into
nothingness, and the coon went
down to the pond
and washed his face and hands and beheld
the world: maybe he didn't:
I am no slave that I
should entertain you, say what you want
to hear, let you wallow in
your silt: one two three four five:
one two three four five six seven eight nine ten:

(all this time I've been
                counting spaces
while you were thinking of something else)
                mess in your own sloppy silt:
                the hounds disappeared
yelping (the way you would at extinction)
                into—the order
                breaks up here—immortality:
I know that's where you think the brave
                little victims should go:
                I do not care what
you think: I do not care what you think:
                I do not care what you
                think: one two three four five
six seven eight nine ten: here we go
                round the here-we-go-round, the
                here-we-go-round, the here-we-
go-round: coon will end in disorder at the
                teeth of hounds: the situation
                will get him:
spheres roll, cubes stay put: now there
                one two three four five
                are two philosophies:
here we go round the mouth-wet of hounds:

                what I choose
                is youse:
                baby

Terrain

The soul is a region without definite boundaries:
    it is not certain a prairie
can exhaust it
        or a range enclose it:
it floats (self-adjusting) like the continental mass,
    where it towers most
extending its deepest mantling base
        (exactly proportional):

does not flow all one way: there is a divide:
  river systems thrown like winter tree-shadows
against the hills: branches, runs, high lakes:
    stagnant lily-marshes:

is variable, has weather: floods unbalancing
  gut it, silt altering the
distribution of weight, the nature of content:
    whirlwinds move through it
or stand spinning like separate orders: the moon comes:
  there are barren spots: bogs, rising
by self-accretion from themselves, a growth into
    destruction of growth,
change of character,
  invasion of peat by poplar and oak: semi-precious
stones and precious metals drop from muddy water into mud:

it is an area of poise, really, held from tipping,
  dark wild water, fierce eels, countercurrents:
a habitat, precise ecology of forms
    mutually to some extent
tolerable, not entirely self-destroying: a crust afloat:
  a scum, foam to the deep and other-natured:
but deeper than depth, too: a vacancy and swirl:

it may be spherical, light and knowledge merely
  the iris and opening
to the dark methods of its sight: how it comes and
    goes, ruptures and heals,
whirls and stands still: the moon comes: terrain.

Unsaid

Have you listened for the things I have left out?
I am nowhere near the end yet and already
      hear
    the hum of omissions,

the chant of vacancies, din of

silences:

there is the other side of matter, antimatter,
    the antiproton:
      we
have measured the proton: it has mass: we
have measured the antiproton: it has negative mass:

you will not

hear me completely even at this early point
unless you hear my emptiness:
    go back:
    how can I
tell you what I have not said: you must look for it

yourself: that

side has weight, too, though words cannot bear it
out: listen for the things I have left out:
    I am
    aware
of them, as you must be, or you will miss

the non-song

in my singing: it is not that words *cannot* say
what is missing: it is only that what is missing
    cannot
    be missed if
spoken: read the parables of my unmaking:

feel the ris-

ing bubble's trembling walls: rush into the domes
these wordy arches shape: hear
    me
    when I am
silent: gather the boundaried vacancies.

Raft

I called the wind and it
went over with me
   to the bluff
      that keeps the sea-bay
and we stayed around for a while
trying to think
      what to do:

I took some time to watch
the tall reeds
and bend their tassels
   over to my touch
      and
as the lowering bay-tide left
      salt-grass
combed flat toward the land
tried to remember
what I came to do:

in the seizures,
I could not think but
      vanished into the beauty
   of any thing I saw
and loved,
pod-stem, cone branch, rocking
      bay grass:

it was almost dark when the wind
breathless from playing
with water
   came over and stopped
resting in the bare trees and dry grass
      and weeds:

I built a fire in a hollow stump
and sitting by

wove a disc of reeds,
  a round raft, and

sometime during the night
  the moon shone but
it must have been the early night
for when I set out
    standing on my disc
and poling with a birch
  it was black dark
of a full tide: the wind slept through my leaving:
I did not wake it to say goodbye:

the raft swirled before day
and the choppy, tugging bay
  let me know
I had caught the tide
and was rushing through

the outer sea-banks
into the open sea:

when dawn came
    I looked
and saw no land:

tide free and
without direction I
gave up the pole,
  my round raft
having no bow,
nowhere to point:

I knelt in the center
to look for where the
    sun would break
and when it started to come
I knew the slow whirl
of my ship
which turned my back to the east

and
brought me slowly round again:

at each revolution
        I had
new glory in my eyes
and thought with chuckles
        where would I be at noon
and what of the night
when the black ocean
might seem not there

though of course stars
        and planets rise and
east can be known
        on a fair night
but I was not
certain
I wanted to go east:
it seemed wise
        to let
the currents be
whatever they would be,
allowing possibility
to chance
where choice
        could not impose itself:

I knelt turning that way
        a long time,
glad I had brought my great
        round hat
for the sun got hot:

at noon
I could not tell
I turned
for overhead the sun,
        motionless in its dome,
spun still
and did not wobble

the dome
or turn a falling shadow
   on my raft's periphery:

soon though that symmetry
eased
    and the sun
was falling
and the wind came
   in an afternoon way

rushing before dark to catch me.

Uh, Philosophy

I understand
   reading the modern philosophers
that truth is so much a method
    it's perfectly all
right for me to believe whatever
   I like or if I like,

nothing:
   I do not know that I care to be set that free:
I am they say
    at liberty to be
provisional, to operate
   expediently, do not have to commit myself

to imperturbables, outright
   legislations, hardfast rules:
they say I can
    prefer my truths,
whatever
   suits my blood,

blends with my proclivities, my temperament:
   I suppose they mean I've had more experience than I can
ever read about, taking in

as I do
possibly a hundred sensations per second, conscious
    and unconscious,

and making a vegetal at least
    synthesis
from them all, so that
        philosophy is
a pry-pole, materialization,
    useful as a snowshovel when it snows:

something solid to knock people down with
    or back people up with:
I do not know that I care to be backed up in just that way:
        the philosophy gives clubs to
everyone, and I prefer disarmament:
    that is, I would rather relate

to the imperturbable objective
    than be the agent of
"possibly unsatisfactory eventualities":
        isn't anything plain true:
if I had something
    to conform to (without responsibility)

I wouldn't feel so hot and sticky:
    (but I must be moved by what I am moved by):
they do say, though, I must give some force to facts,
        must bend that way enough,
be in on the gist of "concrete observations,"
    must be pliant to the drift (roll with the knocks):

they say, too, I must halter my fancy
    mare
with these blinding limitations:
        I don't know that I can go along with that, either:
for though I've proved myself stupid by 33 years
    of getting nowhere,

I must nevertheless be given credit for the sense wherewith
    I decided never to set out:

what are facts if I can't line them up
    anyway I please
and have the freedom
   I refused I think in the beginning?

Sphere

In the dark original water,
amniotic infinity
closed
boundless in circularity:

  tame, heavy
water,
equilibriant,

any will forming to become—
consistency of motion
   arising—
annihilated
by its equal and opposite:

an even, complete extent:
   (there
an eden: how

foreign and far away
your death, rivulets
   trickling
through ripe bowels,

return to heavy water,
infinite multiplicity, in

the deepening, filtering
earthen womb
that bears you forever

beyond
the amnion, O barrier!)

A warm unity, separable but
    entire,
you the nucleus
possessing that universe.

Epiphany

Like a single drop of rain,
    the wasp strikes
the windowpane; buzzes rapidly
away, disguising

error in urgent business:
    such is the
invisible, hard as glass,
unrenderable by the senses,

not known until stricken by:
    some talk that
there is safety in the visible,
the definite, the heard and felt,

pre-stressing the rational and
    calling out with
joy, like people far from death:
how puzzled they will be when

going headlong secure in "things"
    they strike the
intangible and break, lost,
unaccustomed to transparency, to

being without body, energy
    without image:
how they will be dealt
hard realizations, opaque as death.

Muse

From the dark
fragmentations
        build me up
    into a changed brilliant shape,

            realized order,
        mind singing again
    new song, moving into the slow beat and

        disappearing beat
            of perfect resonance:

        how many
times must I be broken and reassembled! anguish of becoming,
        pain of moulting,
    descent! before the unending moment of vision:

    how much disorder must I learn to tolerate
        to find materials
                for the new house of my sight!

        arrange me
        into disorder
    near the breaking of the pattern
    but

            should disorder start to
    tear, the breaking down of possible return,
        oh rise gleaming in recall,

sing me again towering remade, born into a wider
        order, structures deepening,
            inching rootlike into the dark!

Concentrations

I.

By the ocean
dawn is
   more itself,

nets hung like
mist on
   pole-racks or

spread out for mending, weed-picking, corking—

   landreefs of gray
waves
   between the poles:

and the gray
boats, turtle-nosed,
   beached, out

of element, waiting,
salt-bleached,
   keels, hauled

across the sand,
ground to
   wood-ghosts,

sand-ghost gray:
and if there
   is fog,

dawn, becoming itself as reeds, dunes, sheds,

   transfuses it,
opening
   dune-rose-wise

petal by petal—wave, net, boat, oar, thole:

II.

under the reedthatched or pineboughed sheds
dawn men,
opening gray eyes to gray light,

yawn out of the silver nets of dreams
and harden as entities,
their minds hardening the entities they seek:

III.

how you catch a fish, slime-quick
with dart and turn,
loose in the medium:

remove the water,
letting down dams: in pike pools,
maybe looking for bait, dip

the water out,
concentrate the residue, increase
the incidence (you can

catch fry
with your hands then, clutching
the silver lights against the mud:)

if you can't remove
the water, change it, as
by muddying: swamp

ponds yield their fruit to this:
churn up the bottom,
suffocate the brim,

bluegills, "flowers," so they
rise to breathe:
seining

then is good: it
ridding lets the water through,
thickens the impermeables:

(you round-up a tiger,
isolate a compound, the same way:
surrounding, eliminating the habitat and

closing in
on a center or pass
or tiger-run along a river:)

IV.

the men rise from sand and sleep,
    wheel the boat,
strung like a turtle
    under a giant cart,
to the sea's edge:

dropped free,
    the oared boat
leaps, nosing into the surf,
    and spilling
the net astern,
    semicircles back
to land:

hauled in, the net is
    a windrow of fish,
gathered into thin, starving air,
    the ocean, sucking, returned whole
to itself, separation complete,

fish from sea, tiger
    from jungle, vision from experience.

River

I shall
   go down
      to the deep river, to the moonwaters,
where the silver
willows are and the bay blossoms,

to the songs
   of dark birds,
      to the great wooded silence
of flowing
forever down the dark river

silvered at the moon-singing of hidden birds:

27 March

the forsythia is out,
   sprawling like
yellow amoebae, the long
      uneven branches—pseudo-
podia—
   angling on the bottom
of air's spring-clear pool:

shall I
   go down
      to the deep river, to the moonwaters,
where the silver
willows are and the bay blossoms,

to the songs
   of dark birds,
      to the great wooded silence
of flowing
forever down the dark river

silvered at the moon-singing of hidden birds.

Lines

Lines flying in, out: logarithmic
   curves coiling
toward an infinitely inward center: lines
  weaving in, threads lost in clustral scrawl,
   weaving out into loose ends,
wandering beyond the border of gray background,
  going out of vision,
   not returning;
or, returning, breaking across the boundary
  as new lines, discontinuous,
   come into sight:
fiddleheads of ferns, croziers of violins,
  convoluted spherical masses, breaking through
   ditchbanks where briar
stem-dull will
  leave and bloom:
   haunch line, sickle-like, turning down, bulging, nuzzling
under, closing into
  the hidden, sweet, dark meeting of lips:
   the spiralling out
or in
  of galaxies:
   the free-running wavy line, swirling
configuration, halting into a knot
  of curve and density: the broken,
   irreparable filament: tree-winding vines, branching,
falling off or back, free,
  the adventitious preparation for possibility, from
   branch to branch, ash to gum:
the breaker
  hurling into reach for shape, crashing
   out of order, the inner hollow sizzling flat:
the longnecked, uteral gourd, bass line
  continuous in curve,
   melodic line filling and thinning:
concentrations,
  whirling masses,
   thin leaders, disordered ends and risks:

explosions of clusters, expansions from the
   full radial sphere, return's longest chance:
      lines exploring, intersecting, paralleling, twisting,
noding: deranging, clustering.

The Strait

At the oracle
I found the
   god
though active
recalcitrant

unliteral as air:
the priestess
   writhed
and moaned
caught

in the anguish
of some
   perishable
event:
birds flew by:

the urns
hummed: the
   columns
glazed with
sun; on the

inside lit wet with
fire: another, not
   capable
of the inner
speech,

read the priestess
and said,

"The
god wants honor,
desires in you

honor's attitude:
honor him and
    your
venture will
go well:"

cannot, I said,
the god be
    more
specific? will
I honor

him? come again
safe to this
    grove?
the reader said,
"The

descent of the
god is
    awkward,
narrowing and
difficult; first

he is
loose in the
    air,
then captured,
held, by

holy fire: the
circle of columns
    binds
him and from
the columns

the priestess
gathers him,

seized
by her struggling
mouth into

a speech of
forms: it is
     speech
few can read,
the god

violent to
over-reach the
     definite:
why should
he, who is

all, commit
himself to the
     particular?
say himself
into less

than all? pressed
too far, he
     leaves
wounds that are
invisible: it

is only as
she becomes
     him
that the priestess
cannot be hurt

or can be hurt:
should she
     break
her human hold
and go too far

with him,
who could bring

her
back, her eyes
lost to the

visible? step
by step into the
    actual,
truth descending
breaks,

reaches us as
fragmentation
    hardened
into words:"
but, I said, isn't

it convenient
the priestess is
    general
and inexact, merely
turning and wailing?

if the god fails
me, whom shall I
    blame?
her? you who may
have read her wrong?

and if all goes
well, whom shall I
    thank?
the god
with honor,

you with the
actual coin?
    "Night
falls," the reader said,
"the priestess lies

god-torn, limp: the
freed god

flies
again blameless as
air: go

to your fate:
if you succeed, praise the
    god:
if you fail,
discover your flaw."

Open

Exuberance: joy to the last
pained loss
    and hunger of air:
life open, not decided on,
though decided in death:

        the mind cannot be
rid
while it works
    of remembered genitals
beautiful, dank, pliant,

of canyons, brush hills, pastures, streets,
        unities and divisions,
meetings,

exact remembrance of liquid buttocks,
navel, ellipse of hand,

magnified territories of going down
and rising,
the thin tracing saliva line,

    joy's configurations:

serendipity: the unexpected,
the

possible, the unembodied,
              unevented:

the sun will burst: death
is certain: the future limited
    nevertheless is
limitless: the white knotted

    groin,
the finger describing
        entrances!

the dark, warm with glowing awareness, the
hot dis-
      missals of desire
until the last last tear of pain:

until the end nothing ends, lust
forward, rushing;
      pillars of ice wet-bright in melt,
warm

with always-yielding joy: yes
      yes
yes, the loose mouths hiss in the mornings of death.

Catalyst

Honor the maggot,
      supreme catalyst:
he spurs the rate of change:
(all scavengers are honorable: I love them
all,
will scribble hard as I can for them)

      he accelerates change
      in the changeless continuum;
where the body falls completed, he sets to work:
where the spirit attains
    indifference

he makes his residence:
in the egg on wing from mound
to mound he travels,
feeds, finds his wings,

      after the wet-sweet of decay,
      after the ant-sucked earth has drunk
      the honey-fluids,
      after
      the veins
   lie dried to streaks of tendon
      inside the meat-free, illuminated skull,

lofts, saws the air, copulates in a hung
rapture
of riding, holds the sweet-clear
connection
      through dual flights, male and female,
      soil's victory:
      (dead cell dross transfigured
      into gloss,
   iridescence of compound eyes,
duck-neck purple of hairy abdomen)

      O worm supreme,
transformer of bloated, breaking flesh
into colorless netted wings,
into the wills of sex and song, leaving
   ash on odorless ground, the scent
      of pinestraw
rising dominant from the striking sun!

Christmas Eve

When cold, I huddle up, foetal, cross
arms:
but in summer, sprawl:

  secret is plain old
surface area,

decreased in winter, retaining: in summer no
     limbs touching—
radiating:
everything is physical:

     chemistry is physical:
     electrical noumenal mind
   is:
(I declare!)

put up Christmas tree this afternoon:
     fell
asleep in big chair: woke up at
3:12 and it
     was snowing outside, was white!

Christmas Eve tonight: Joseph
is looking for a place:
Mary smiles but
     her blood is singing:

     she will have to lie down:
   hay is warm:
some inns keep only
the public room warm: Mary

is thinking, Nice time
     to lie down,
good time to be brought down by this necessity:

I better get busy
and put the lights on—can't find
     extension cord:
Phyllis will be home, will say, The
tree doesn't have any lights!
I have tiny winking lights, too:
     she will like
them: she went to see her mother:

my mother is dead: she is
deep in the ground, changed: if she

rises, dust will blow all over the place and
   she will stand there shining,
smiling: she will feel good:
she will want
to go home and fix supper: first she
     will hug me:

an actual womb bore Christ,
divinity into the world:
   I hope there are births to lie down to
back
to divinity,
since we all must die away from here:

I better look for the cord:
we're going to
     the Plaza for dinner:
tonight, a buffet: tomorrow there, we'll
   have a big Christmas
dinner:

before I fell asleep, somebody
phoned, a Mr. Powell: he asked
    if I wanted to
sell my land
in Mays Landing: I don't know:
I have several pieces, wonder
   if he wants them all,
wonder what I ought to quote:

earth: so many acres of earth:
own:
how we own who are owned! well,
anyway, he won't care
     about that—said he would
call back Monday: I will
tell him something then:
   it's nearly Christmas, now:
they are all going into the city:
some have sent ahead for reservations:
the inns are filling up:

Christ was born
in a hay barn among the warm cows and the
donkeys kneeling down: with Him divinity
swept into the flesh
and made it real.

Identity

1)   An individual spider web
identifies a species:

an order of instinct prevails
through all accidents of circumstance,
though possibility is
high along the peripheries of
spider

webs:
you can go all
around the fringing attachments

and find
disorder ripe,
entropy rich, high levels of random,
numerous occasions of accident:

2)   the possible settings
of a web are infinite:

how does
the spider keep
identity
while creating the web
in a particular place?

how and to what extent
and by what modes of chemistry
and control?

it is
wonderful

             how things work: I will tell you
                          about it
                          because

it is interesting
and because whatever is
moves in weeds
        and stars and spider webs
and known
                    is loved:
                    in that love,
                    each of us knowing it,
                    I love you,

for it moves within and beyond us,
              sizzles in
winter grasses, darts and hangs with bumblebees
by summer windowsills:

                   I will show you
the underlying that takes no image to itself,
              cannot be shown or said,
but weaves in and out of moons and bladderweeds,
              is all and
         beyond destruction
         because created fully in no
particular form:

                   if the web were perfectly pre-set,
                   the spider could
         never find
         a perfect place to set it in: and

                   if the web were
perfectly adaptable,
if freedom and possibility were without limit,
                   the web would
lose its special identity:

         the row-strung garden web
keeps order at the center

where space is freest (interesting that the freest
        "medium" should
            accept the firmest order)

and that
order
            diminishes toward the
periphery
        allowing at the points of contact
                entropy equal to entropy.

What This Mode of Motion Said

        You will someday
try to prove me wrong
(I am the wings when you me fly)
to replace me with some mode
        you made
and think is right:

            I am the way by
            which you prove me
                wrong,
            the reason you
            reason against me:

I change shape,
turn easily into the shapes you make
        and even you
            in moving
I leave, betray:

what has not yet been imagined has been
imagined by me
        whom you honor, reach for—
change unending though
slowed into nearly limited modes:

        question me and I

     will give you an answer

narrow and definite
as the question
        that devours you (the exact

is a conquest of time that time vanquishes)
     or vague as wonder
by which I elude you:

      pressed
      for certainty
I harden to a stone,
lie unimaginable in meaning
     at your feet,

      leave you less
certainty than you brought, leave
     you to create the stone
as any image of yourself,
shape of your dreams:

      pressed too far
I wound, returning endless
inquiry
for the pride of inquiry:

      shapeless, unspendable,
     powerless in the actual
     which I rule, I

     will not
make deposits in your bank account
or free you from bosses
      in little factories,
will not spare you insult, will not
protect you from
men who
     have never heard of modes, who
do not respect me
or your knowledge of me in you;

> men I let win,
> their thin tight lips
> humiliating my worshippers:
>
> I betray
> him who gets me in his eyes and sees
> beyond the fact
> to the motions of my permanence.

Nucleus

How you buy a factory:
    got wind of one for sale in

Montreal,
        Hochelaga
        where Cartier, amicably received,
    gave the squaws and children

tin bells and tin paternosters
and the men knives
        and went up to the nearby
height and
        called it Mt. Royal
from which the view was
panoramic,
        an island 17 x 40
miles,
        good trees (good as France)
        and, below, thick maize:

Montreal,
    got "The Laurentian" out of New York
first morning after the strike ended
and rode up parlor-car (expense account)
        along the solid-white Hudson
        and on up into hilled
graybirch country, through the Adirondacks
and along the high west bank of Lake Champlain

      (on heavy ice
    men in windhuts fishing)

      and read Bottom
    and "gives to airy nothing
A local habitation and a name":

      met the vice president
in the lobby at 8 next morning, ascended
étage de confrères, troisième étage, s'il vous plaît,
      third floor, please)
to the 22nd floor
      to "The Panorama"
for breakfast: sight to see: St. Lawrence over there,
Windsor Hotel remodeling, where the Queen stayed,
      cathedral, replica (but smaller)
        of St. Peter's:

Montreal,
and left center city by cab,
      through the French Quarter, out near Westmont,
long stairs from street to second floor,
      said it was typical,
with metal viny rails,

      and on through streets, bilingual
traffic signs, turn left, left again: there:
Linden Street: 807, a local habitation and a name,

four walls, a limited, defined, exact place,
      a nucleus,
solidification from possibility:

      how you buy a factory:
determine the lines of
force
leading in and out, origins, destinations of lines;
determine how
     from the nexus of crossed and bundled lines
      the profit is
obtained, the

forces realized, the cheap made dear,
and whether the incoming or outgoing forces are stronger
and exactly why,
and what is to be done:

    raw material inventory is
in winter
high: river frozen, must make half-year provisions,
squirrel-like, last till thaw, is
a warehousing problem: comes from England,
          Germany (West):
             important to keep a ready
stock of finished goods—customers won't wait, will
order from parent companies in England, Germany:

    property taxes: things are
changing, you may get a rail siding here soon:
      profit and loss sheet, cash flow, receivables:
      large lot, vacancy providing for the future:
good machineshop and
          here are the production lines:
how many heads on those machines: pcs per hr:
          wages, skilled
unskilled: cut-off machines, annealing ovens, formers:
    "I'll say! 15 below this morning."

order backlog: "I would say we have
    an edge,
growth possibility: 50 good customers, pharm-
aceutical houses: you have to understand the background."
    Perspective.

"Eight years ago . . . finally, I had to go to
Ottawa . . . left good man here, Oh, yes, he's done
fine . . . Swiss, later in Johannesburg;
    you understand, management
          wouldn't consider
selling him out, too much of himself:" un-

favorable points: competition, international market,
low tariffs,

unprotected, only advantage personalized service
        to local
accounts, could
                buy elsewhere,
large firms in States have bigger machines, faster,
more production per hour

(more overhead, too)

"being small's our advantage . . . can adapt, work with
short runs of specialities—customers want
                their own designs, premium,
made-to-order prices . . ."

Montreal,
        "sure to see McGill U., ice sculpture front of
each dorm, emblem"
cornless lawns,
                Cartier going through the motions of worship,
Indians looking up at sky, too,
can't see what:

"We'll get that information to you"
                further study
and in the deep cold night boarding train, bedroom,
Yassuh,
and heat connections broken, cold, next morning
                going uptrain for toast and coffee,
that's where East River turns—Manhattan:
lines of force, winding, unwinding,
        nexus coiling in the mind:
                balance, judge: act:

Jungle Knot

    One morning Beebe
        found on a bank of the Amazon
    an owl and snake
            dead in a coiled embrace:

the vine prints its coil too deep into the tree
and leaved fire shoots greens of tender flame
        rising among the branches,
drawing behind a hardening, wooden clasp:

the tree does not
        generally escape
though it may live thralled for years,
    succumbing finally rather than at once,

        in the vine's victory
the casting of its eventual death,
    though it may live years
on the skeletal trunk,

termites rising, the rain softening,
    a limb in storm
falling, the vine air-free at last, structureless as death:
    the owl,

    Beebe says, underestimated
the anaconda's size: hunger had deformed
        sight or caution, or
anaconda, come out in moonlight on the river bank,

had left half his length in shade: (you
        sometimes tackle
more than just what the light shows):
    the owl struck talons

        back of the anaconda's head
but weight grounded him in surprise: the anaconda
    coiled, embracing heaving wings
and cry, and the talons, squeezed in, sank

killing snake and owl in tightened pain:
    errors of vision, errors of self-defense!
errors of wisdom, errors of desire!
        the vulture dives, unlocks four eyes.

The Misfit

The unassimilable fact leads us on:
round the edges
  where broken shapes make poor masonry
the synthesis
fails (and succeeds) into limitation
  or extending itself too far

becomes a different synthesis:
law applies
  consistently to the molecule,
not to the ocean, unoriented, unprocessed,
it floats in, that floats in it:
  we are led on

to the boundaries
where relations loosen into chaos
  or where the nucleus fails to control,
fragments in odd shapes
expressing more and more the interstitial sea:
  we are led on

to peripheries, to the raw blocks of material,
where mortar and trowel can convert
  diversity into enlarging unity:
not the million oriented facts
but the one or two facts,
  out of place,

recalcitrant, the one observed fact
that tears us into questioning:
  what has not
joined dies into order to redeem, with
loss of singleness extends the form,
  or, unassimilable, leads us on.

Nelly Myers

I think of her
            while having a bowl of wheatflakes
(why? we never had wheatflakes
or any cereal then
except breakfast grits)
                  and tears come to my eyes
and I think that I will die
because

      the bright, clear days when she was with me
and when we were together
(without caring that we were together)

can never be restored:
            my love wide-ranging
   I mused with clucking hens
and brought in from summer storms
at midnight the thrilled cold chicks
                  and dried them out
                  at the fireplace
and got up before morning
unbundled them from the piles of rags and
   turned them into the sun:

      I cannot go back
         I cannot be with her again

            and my love included the bronze
sheaves of broomstraw
she would be coming across the fields with
before the household was more than stirring out to pee

and there she would be coming
   as mysteriously from a new world
and she was already old when I was born but I love

the thought of her hand
wringing the tall tuft of dried grass

        and I cannot see her beat out the fuzzy bloom
again
readying the straw for our brooms at home,
I can never see again the calm sentence of her mind
   as she
measured out brooms for the neighbors and charged
a nickel a broom:

I think of her
   but cannot remember how I thought of her
as I grew up: she was not a member of the family:
I knew she was not my mother,
              not an aunt, there was nothing
visiting about her: she had her room,
     she kept her bag of money
(on lonely Saturday afternoons
   you could sometimes hear the coins
spilling and spilling into her apron):
     she never went away, she was Nelly Myers, we
     called her Nel,
small, thin, her legs wrapped from knees to ankles
in homespun bandages: she always had the soreleg
                            and sometimes
red would show at the knee, or the ankle would swell
and look hot
     (and sometimes the cloths would
dwindle,
     the bandages grow thin, the bowed legs look
pale and dry—I would feel good then,
        maybe for weeks
              there would seem reason of promise,
     though she rarely mentioned her legs
and was rarely asked about them): she always went,

legs red or white, went, went
through the mornings before sunrise
              covering the fields and
woods

looking for huckleberries
or quieting some wild call to move and go
        roaming the woods and acres of daybreak
and there was always a fire in the stove
when my mother rose (which was not late):

    my grandmother, they say, took her in
when she was a stripling run away from home
(her mind was not perfect
        which is no bar to this love song
                for her smile was sweet,
    her outrage honest and violent)
and they say that after she worked all day her relatives
would throw a handful of dried peas into her lap
                    for her supper
and she came to live in the house I was born in the
northwest room of:

oh I will not end my grief
        that she is gone, I will not end my singing;
my songs like blueberries
felt-out and black to her searching fingers before light
welcome her
wherever her thoughts ride with mine, now or in any time
    that may come
when I am gone; I will not end visions of her naked feet
in the sandpaths: I will hear her words
        "Applecandy" which meant Christmas,
"Lambesdamn" which meant Goddamn (she was forthright
        and didn't go to church
    and nobody wondered if she should

and I agree with her the Holcomb pinegrove bordering our
field was
more hushed and lovelier than cathedrals
    not to mention country churches with unpainted boards
and so much innocence as she carried in her face
has entered few churches in one person)

and her exclamation "Founshy-day!" I know no meaning for

but knew she was using it right:

and I will not forget how though nearly deaf
she heard the tender blood in lips of children
and knew the hurt
 and knew what to do:

and I will not forget how I saw her last, tied in a chair
lest she rise to go
and fall
   for how innocently indomitable
 was her lust
and how her legs were turgid with still blood as she sat
and how real her tears were as I left
 to go back to college (damn all colleges):
  oh where her partial soul, as others thought,
roams roams my love,
mother, not my mother, grandmother, not my grandmother,
slave to our farm's work, no slave I would not stoop to:
I will not end my grief, earth will not end my grief,
I move on, we move on, some scraps of us together,
 my broken soul leaning toward her to be touched,
listening to be healed.

Motion for Motion

 Watched on the sandy, stony bottom of the stream
 the oval black shadow of the waterbeetle, shadow

 larger than beetle, though no blacker, mirroring
 at a down and off angle motion for motion, whirl, run:

   (if I knew the diameters
   of oval and beetle, the
   depth of the stream, several
    indices of refraction
    and so forth

   I might say why

the shadow outsizes the
beetle—

I admit to mystery
in the obvious—

but now that I remember some
I think the shadow
included the bent water where
the beetle rode, surface

tension, not breaking, bending
under to hold him up,

the deformation recorded in shade:
for light, arising from so far away,

is parallel
through a foot of water
(though edge-light
would

make a difference—a beetle can
exist among such differences
and do well):

someone has a clear vision of it all,
exact to complete existence;
loves me when I swear and praise
and smiles, probably, to see me
wrestle with sight

and gain no reason from it, or money,
but a blurred mind overexposed):

caught the sudden gust of a catbird, selfshot
under the bridge and out into my sight: he splashed
into the air near a briervine, lit:

I don't know by what will: it was clear sailing
on down the stream

and prettier—a moss-bright island made two streams
and then made one and, farther, two fine birches
and a lot of things to see: but he stopped

back to me,
didn't see me, hopped on through the vines, by some
will not including me . . .

and then there were two beetles, and later three at
once swimming in the sun, and three shadows,
all reproduced, multiplied without effort
or sound, the unique beetle—and I—lost to an

automatic machinery in things, duplicating, without
useful difference, some changeless order extending
backward beyond the origin of earth,

changeless and true, even before the water fell, or
the sun broke, or the beetle turned, or the still
human head bent from a bridge-rail above to have a look.

Visit

It is not far to my place:
you can come smallboat,
pausing under shade in the eddies
    or going ashore
        to rest, regard the leaves

    or talk with birds and
shore weeds: hire a full grown man not
late in years to oar you
    and choose a canoe-like thin ship:
        (a dumb man is better and no

    costlier; he will attract
the reflections and silences under leaves:)
travel light: a single book, some twine:

the river is muscled at rapids with trout
  and a birch limb

will make a suitable spit: if you
leave in the forenoon, you will arrive
with plenty of light
  the afternoon of the third day: I will
    come down to the landing

(tell your man to look for it,
the dumb have clear sight and are free of
visions) to greet you with some made
  wine and a special verse:
    or you can come by shore:

choose the right: there the rocks
cascade less frequently, the grade more gradual:
treat yourself gently: the ascent thins both
  mind and blood and you must
    keep still a dense reserve

of silence we can poise against
conversation: there is little news:
I found last month a root with shape and
  have heard a new sound among
    the insects: come.

Four Motions for the Pea Vines

I.

the rhythm is
  diffusion and concentration:
in and out:
          expansion and
contraction: the unfolding,
  furling:

        the forces
        that propel the rhythm,

the lines of winding-up,
loosening, depositing,
  dissolving:

the vehicles!

light, the vehicle of itself, light
surrounding
we are made and fed by:
water, the solvent, vehicle
of molecules and grains,
the dissolver and depositor,
the maker of films
and residues,
the all-absorbing vessel uncontained!

        the rhythm is
        out and
        in,
        diffusion and concentration:

        the dry pea from the
        ground
        expands to vines and leaves,
        harvests sun and water
        into
        baby-white new peas:

the forms that exist
in this rhythm! the whirling
  forms!
  grief and glory of
this rhythm:
the rhythm is

                    2.

for the expansions (and concentrations) here
is the five-acre
  Todd Field:

seeding, too, is gathering,
preparation to collect

    mineral, rain, and light, and
between the corn-rows,
the broadcast field peas
fall into soft, laying-by soil:

    dry beads of concentration
            covered by the moist
general ground:

and the general moisture, the rain's
held shadow, softens, breaks
down, swells
and frees
            the hard incipience that
generalizes outward toward extension;
the root reaching with gravity,
the stalk opposing
crazing through the black land upward to the light

                        3.

fat and sassy
    the raucous crows
    along the wood's edge
    trouble the tops of
yellowing pines
    with points of dipping black;

cluster into groups
from summer,
    the younglings in their wings
poised,
careful,
    precise,

the dazed awkwardness of heavy nest birds
hardened lean into grace;

assemble along the edge of the field and
            begin winter talk,

remembrances of summer and separations,
  agree
  or disagree
      on a roost,
      the old birds more often silent,

calmer and more tolerant in their memory,
    wiser of dangers
  experienced or conceived,
  less inclined to play,
  irritable,
      but at times

exultant in pitched flight,
as if catching for a moment
  youth's inexperienced gladness, or as if
      feeling
      over time and danger
      a triumph greater than innocent joy:

to turn aside and live with them
  would not seem
      much different—

each of us going into winter with gains and losses,
dry, light peas of concentration nearby
  (for a winter's gleaning)
      to expand warmth through us

4.

slow as the pale low-arcing sun, the women move
  down windy rows of the autumn field:
the peavines are dead:
cornstalks and peapods rattle in the dry bleach
      of cold:

the women glean remnant peas
  (too old to snap or shell) that

got past being green; shatter from skeletal vines
    handfuls of peapods, tan, light:

bent the slow women drag towsacks huge
    with peas, bulk but little
weight: a boy carries a sack on his
    shoulders to the end of the rows:
he stoops: the sack goes over his head

to the ground: he flails it with a tobacco stick,
    opens the sack, removes the husks, and
from sack to tub winnows
    dry hard crackling peas: rhythms reaching through
seasons, motions weaving in and out!

Expressions of Sea Level

Peripherally the ocean
marks itself
    against the gauging land
it erodes and
builds:

it is hard to name
the changeless:
speech without words,
    silence renders it:
and mid-ocean,

sky sealed unbroken to sea,
    there is no way to know
the ocean's speech,
intervolved and markless,
breaking against

    no boulder-held fingerland:
broken, surf things are expressions:
the sea speaks far from its core,

far from its center relinquishes the
long-held roar:

of any mid-sea
speech, the yielding resistances
of wind and water, spray,
swells, whitecaps, moans,
    it is a dream the sea makes,

an inner problem, a self-deep
dark and private anguish
    revealed in small,
by hints, to
keen watchers on the shore:

only with the staid land
is the level conversation really held:
only in the meeting of rock and
    sea is
hard relevance shattered into light:

upbeach the clam shell
    holds smooth dry sand,
remembrance of tide:
water can go at
least that high: in

    the night, if you stay
to watch, or
if you come tomorrow at the right time,
you can see the shell caught
again in wash, the

sand turbulence changed,
new sand left smooth: if
the shell washes loose,
flops over,
    buries its rim in flux,

it will not be silence for
a shell that spoke: the

half-buried back will
tell how the ocean dreamed
breakers against the land:

into the salt marshes the water comes fast with rising tide:
an inch of rise spreads by yards
    through tidal creeks, round fingerways of land:
the marsh grasses stem-logged
combine wind and water motions,
    slow from dry trembling
to heavier motions of wind translated through
cushioned stems; tide-held slant of grasses
    bent into the wind:

    is there a point of rest where
    the tide turns: is there one
    infinitely tiny higher touch
on the legs of egrets, the
skin of back, bay-eddy reeds:
    is there an instant when fullness is,
    without loss, complete: is there a
    statement perfect in its speech:

how do you know the moon
is moving: see the dry
casting of the beach worm
    dissolve at the
delicate rising touch:

that is the
    expression of sea level.
the talk of giants,
of ocean, moon, sun, of everything,
spoken in a dampened grain of sand.

Discoverer

If you must leave the shores of mind,
scramble down the walls

of dome-locked underwater caves
into the breathless, held

clarity of dark, where no waves break,
a grainy, colloidal grist
and quiet, carry a light: carry $A = \pi r^2$,
carry Kepler's equal areas in

equal times: as air line take Baudelaire's
L'Albatros: as depth markers
to call you back, fix the words of
the golden rule: feed the

night of your seeking with clusters
of ancient light:
remember the sacred sheaf, the rods of
civilization, the holy

bundle of elements: if to cast light
you must enter diffusion's ruin,
carry with you light to cast, to
gather darkness by: carry A is to B

as A plus B is to A: if to gather darkness
into light, evil into good,
you must leave the shores of mind,
remember us, return and rediscover us.

Event

A leaf fallen is
fallen
throughout the universe
and
from the instant of
its fall, for
all time gone
and to come:

worlds jiggle in
webs, drub

in leaf lakes,
squiggle in
drops of ditchwater:

size and place
begin, end,
time is allowed
in event's instant:
away or
at home, universe and
leaf try
to fall: occur.

One:Many

To maintain balance
between one and many by
        keeping in operation both one and many:

        fear a too great consistency, an arbitrary
imposition
        from the abstract *one*
        downwardly into the realities of manyness:
    this makes unity
not deriving from the balance of manyness
but by destruction of diversity:
    it is unity
            unavailable to change,
cut off from the reordering possibilities of
        variety:

            when I tried to summarize
            a moment's events
along the creek shore this afternoon,
the tide gathering momentum outwardly,
terns
hovering
dropping to spear shallow water,
    the minnows
in a band

wavering between deep and shallow water,
the sand hissing
into new images,
       the grass at its sound and symmetry,
       scoring
       semicircles of wind
  into sand,
the tan beetle in a footprint dead,
flickering to
  gusts of wind,
       the bloodsucking flies
       at their song and savage whirl,
when I tried to think by what
millions of grains of events
  the tidal creek had altered course,
    when I considered alone
a record
of the waves on the running blue creek,
  I was released into a power beyond my easy failures,
released to think
how so much freedom
    can keep the broad look of serenity
    and nearly statable balance:

not unity by the winnowing out of difference,
not unity thin and substanceless as abstraction,
  uneventful as theory:

I think of California's towns and ranges,
  deserts and oil fields,
highways, forests, white boulders,
    valleys, shorelines,
    headlands of rock;
and of Maine's
    unpainted seahouses
    way out on the tips of fingerlands,
lobster traps and pots,
freshwater lakes; of Chicago,
  hung like an eggsac on the leaf of Lake
Michigan, with
its

Art Museum, Prudential Building, Knickerbocker Hotel
(where Cummings stayed);
of North Carolina's
Pamlico and Albemarle Sounds, outer banks, shoals,
     telephone wire loads of swallows,
of Columbus County
          where fresh-dug peanuts
          are boiled
          in iron pots, salt filtering
in through boiled-clean shells (a delicacy
true
as artichokes or Jersey
asparagus): and on and on through the villages,
along dirt roads, ditchbanks, by gravel pits and on
     to the homes, to the citizens and their histories,
inventions, longings:
I think how enriching, though unassimilable as a whole
into art, are the differences: the small-business
man in
          Kansas City declares an extra dividend
and his daughter
          who teaches school in Duquesne
buys a Volkswagen, a second car for the family:
out of many, one:
from variety an over-riding unity, the expression of
variety:

no book of laws, short of unattainable reality itself,
can anticipate every event,
control every event: only the book of laws founded
     against itself,
founded on freedom of each event to occur as itself,
lasts into the inevitable balances events will take.

Still

    I said I will find what is lowly
          and put the roots of my identity
          down there:
    each day I'll wake up

and find the lowly nearby,
        a handy focus and reminder,
a ready measure of my significance,
the voice by which I would be heard,
the wills, the kinds of selfishness
        I could
freely adopt as my own:

but though I have looked everywhere,
        I can find nothing
        to give myself to:
        everything is

magnificent with existence, is in
surfeit of glory:
nothing is diminished,
nothing has been diminished for me:

I said what is more lowly than the grass:
        ah, underneath,
        a ground-crust of dry-burnt moss:
        I looked at it closely
and said this can be my habitat: but
nestling in I
found
        below the brown exterior
        green mechanisms beyond intellect
awaiting resurrection in rain: so I got up

and ran saying there is nothing lowly in the universe:
I found a beggar:
he had stumps for legs: nobody was paying
him any attention: everybody went on by:
        I nestled in and found his life:
there, love shook his body like a devastation:
I said
        though I have looked everywhere
        I can find nothing lowly
        in the universe:

I whirled through transfigurations up and down,
transfigurations of size and shape and place:

at one sudden point came still,
stood in wonder:
moss, beggar, weed, tick, pine, self, magnificent
with being!

The Yucca Moth

The yucca clump
is blooming,
    tall sturdy spears
spangling into bells of light,
    green
in the white blooms
    faint as
a memory of mint:

I raid
    a bloom,
spread the hung petals out,
    and, surprised he is not
a bloom-part, find
    a moth inside, the exact color,
the bloom his daylight port or cove:

though time comes
    and goes and troubles
are unlessened,
    the yucca is lifting temples
of bloom: from the night
    of our dark flights, can
we go in to heal, live
    out in white-green shade
the radiant, white, hanging day?

Two Motions

I.

It is not enough to be willing to come out of the dark
    and stand in the light,
all hidden things brought into sight, the damp
  black spaces,
where fear, arms over its head, trembles into blindness,
    invaded by truth-seeking light:
it is not enough to desire radiance, to be struck by
  radiance: external light
throws darkness behind its brilliance, the division
    nearly half and half:
it is only enough when the inner light
  kindles to a source, radiates from its sphere to all
points outwardly: then, though
    surrounding things are half and half with
light and darkness, all that is visible from the source
  is light:
it is not enough to wish to cast light: as much
    darkness as light is made that way: it is only
enough to touch the inner light of each surrounding thing
  and hope it will itself be stirred to radiance,
eliminating the shadows that all lights give it,
    and realizing its own full sphere:
it is only enough to radiate the sufficient light
  within, the
constant source, the light beyond all possibility of night.

II.

  However;

      in separating light from darkness
        have we cast into death:
      in attaining the luminous,
   made, capable self,
      have we
        brought error
  to perfection:

in naming have we divided what
    unnaming will not undivide:

in coming so far,
synthesizing, enlarging, incorporating, completing
(all the way to a finished Fragment)
    have we foundered into arrival:

in tarring, calking, timbering,
    have we kept our ship afloat
        only to satisfy all destinations
by no departures;
        only to abandon helm,
sailcloth, hemp, spar;
        only to turn charts
to weather, compass to salt, sextant
    to sea:

as far as words will let us go, we have
        voyaged: now
we disperse the ruin of our gains
to do a different kind of going
that will
become less and
less
voyaging

        as arrival approaches nowhere-everywhere
        in gain of nothing-everything.

The Constant

When leaving the primrose, bayberry dunes, seaward
I discovered the universe this morning,
        I was in no
mood
for wonder,
        the naked mass of so much miracle

already beyond the vision
of my grasp:

along a rise of beach, a hundred feet from the surf,
a row of clam shells
    four to ten feet wide
    lay sinuous as far as sight:

in one shell—though in the abundance
            there were others like it—upturned,
four or five inches across the wing,
a lake
three to four inches long and two inches wide,
all dimensions rounded,
    indescribable in curve:

and on the lake a turning galaxy, a film of sand,
co-ordinated, nearly circular (no real perfections),
    an inch in diameter, turning:
turning:
counterclockwise, the wind hardly perceptible from 11 o'clock
        with noon at sea:
        the galaxy rotating,
        but also,
at a distance from the shell lip,
revolving
round and round the shell:

        a gull's toe could spill the universe:
two more hours of sun could dry it up:
a higher wind could rock it out:

the tide will rise, engulf it, wash it loose:
utterly:

the terns, their
    young somewhere hidden in clumps of grass or weed,
were diving *sshik sshik* at me,
        then pealing upward for another round and dive:

I have had too much of this inexhaustible miracle:
miracle, this massive, drab constant of experience.

Motion

The word is
not the thing:
is
a construction of,
a tag for,
the thing: the
word in
no way
resembles
the thing, except
as sound
resembles,
as in *whirr*,
sound:
the relation
between what this
as words
is
and what is
is tenuous: we
agree upon
this as the net to
cast on what
is: the finger
to
point with: the
method of
distinguishing,
defining, limiting:
poems
are fingers, methods,
nets,
not what is or
was:
but the music
in poems
is different,
points to nothing,

traps no
realities, takes
no game, but
by the motion of
its motion
resembles
what, moving, is—
the wind
underleaf white against
the tree.

WCW

I turned in
by the bayshore
and parked,
the crosswind
hitting me hard
side the head,
the bay scrappy
and working:
what a
way to read
Williams! till
a woman came
and turned
her red dog loose
to sniff
(and piss
on)
the dead horseshoe
crabs.

Corsons Inlet

I went for a walk over the dunes again this morning
to the sea,

then turned right along
   the surf
           rounded a naked headland
           and returned

   along the inlet shore:

it was muggy sunny, the wind from the sea steady and high,
crisp in the running sand,
     some breakthroughs of sun
   but after a bit

continuous overcast:

the walk liberating, I was released from forms,
from the perpendiculars,
     straight lines, blocks, boxes, binds
of thought
into the hues, shadings, rises, flowing bends and blends
       of sight:

            I allow myself eddies of meaning:
yield to a direction of significance
running
like a stream through the geography of my work:
  you can find
in my sayings
          swerves of action
          like the inlet's cutting edge:
      there are dunes of motion,
organizations of grass, white sandy paths of remembrance
in the overall wandering of mirroring mind:

but Overall is beyond me: is the sum of these events
I cannot draw, the ledger I cannot keep, the accounting
beyond the account:

in nature there are few sharp lines: there are areas of
primrose
    more or less dispersed;
disorderly orders of bayberry; between the rows

of dunes,
irregular swamps of reeds,
though not reeds alone, but grass, bayberry, yarrow, all . . .
predominantly reeds:

I have reached no conclusions, have erected no boundaries,
shutting out and shutting in, separating inside
>from outside: I have
>drawn no lines:
>as

manifold events of sand
change the dune's shape that will not be the same shape
tomorrow,

so I am willing to go along, to accept
the becoming
thought, to stake off no beginnings or ends, establish
>no walls:

by transitions the land falls from grassy dunes to creek
to undercreek: but there are no lines, though
>change in that transition is clear
>as any sharpness: but "sharpness" spread out,
allowed to occur over a wider range
than mental lines can keep:

the moon was full last night: today, low tide was low:
black shoals of mussels exposed to the risk
of air
and, earlier, of sun,
waved in and out with the waterline, waterline inexact,
caught always in the event of change:
>a young mottled gull stood free on the shoals
>and ate
to vomiting: another gull, squawking possession, cracked a crab,
picked out the entrails, swallowed the soft-shelled legs, a ruddy
turnstone running in to snatch leftover bits:

risk is full: every living thing in
siege: the demand is life, to keep life: the small

white blacklegged egret, how beautiful, quietly stalks and spears
          the shallows, darts to shore
                    to stab—what? I couldn't
          see against the black mudflats—a frightened
          fiddler crab?

               the news to my left over the dunes and
reeds and bayberry clumps was
               fall: thousands of tree swallows
               gathering for flight:
               an order held
               in constant change: a congregation
rich with entropy: nevertheless, separable, noticeable
          as one event,
                    not chaos: preparations for
flight from winter,
cheet, cheet, cheet, cheet, wings rifling the green clumps,
beaks
at the bayberries
     a perception full of wind, flight, curve,
     sound:
     the possibility of rule as the sum of rulelessness:
the "field" of action
with moving, incalculable center:

in the smaller view, order tight with shape:
blue tiny flowers on a leafless weed: carapace of crab:
snail shell:
          pulsations of order
          in the bellies of minnows: orders swallowed,
broken down, transferred through membranes
to strengthen larger orders: but in the large view, no
lines or changeless shapes: the working in and out, together
          and against, of millions of events: this,
                    so that I make
                    no form
                    formlessness:

orders as summaries, as outcomes of actions override
or in some way result, not predictably (seeing me gain
the top of a dune,

the swallows
could take flight—some other fields of bayberry
        could enter fall
        berryless) and there is serenity:

        no arranged terror: no forcing of image, plan,
or thought:
no propaganda, no humbling of reality to precept:

terror pervades but is not arranged, all possibilities
of escape open: no route shut, except in
    the sudden loss of all routes:

        I see narrow orders, limited tightness, but will
not run to that easy victory:
        still around the looser, wider forces work:
        I will try
    to fasten into order enlarging grasps of disorder, widening
scope, but enjoying the freedom that
Scope eludes my grasp, that there is no finality of vision,
that I have perceived nothing completely,
        that tomorrow a new walk is a new walk.

Saliences

        Consistencies rise
        and ride
        the mind down
        hard routes
            walled
        with no outlet and so
        to open a variable geography,
            proliferate
        possibility, here
        is this dune fest
            releasing
        mind feeding out,
        gathering clusters,
        fields of order in disorder,

where choice
can make beginnings,
    turns,
    reversals,
where straight line
and air-hard thought
can meet
unarranged disorder,
    dissolve
before the one event that
creates present time
in the multi-variable
    scope:
a variable of wind
among the dunes,
making variables
of position and direction and sound
of every reed leaf
and bloom,
running streams of sand,
winding, rising, at a depression
falling out into deltas,
weathering shells with blast,
striking hiss into clumps of grass,
against bayberry leaves,
    lifting
the spider from footing to footing
hard across the dry even crust
toward the surf:
wind, a variable, soft wind, hard
steady wind, wind
shaped and kept in the
bent of trees,
the prevailing dipping seaward
of reeds,
the kept and erased sandcrab trails:
wind, the variable to the gull's flight,
how and where he drops the clam
and the way he heads in, running to loft:
wind, from the sea, high surf
and cool weather;
from the land, a lessened breakage

and the land's heat:
wind alone as a variable,
as a factor in millions of events,
leaves no two moments
on the dunes the same:
   keep
free to these events,
bend to these
changing weathers:
multiple as sand, events of sense
alter old dunes
of mind,
release new channels of flow,
free materials
to new forms:
wind alone as a variable
takes this neck of dunes
out of calculation's reach:
come out of the hard
routes and ruts,
pour over the walls
of previous assessments: turn to
the open,
the unexpected, to new saliences of feature.

*

The reassurance is
that through change
continuities sinuously work,
cause and effect
   without alarm,
gradual shadings out or in,
motions that full
   with time
do not surprise, no
abrupt leap or burst: possibility,
with meaningful development
of circumstance:

when I went back to the dunes today,
   saliences,
congruent to memory,

spread firmingly across my sight:
the narrow white path
rose and dropped over
grassy rises toward the sea:
sheets of reeds,
tasseling now near fall,
filled the hollows
with shapes of ponds or lakes:
bayberry, darker, made wandering
chains of clumps, sometimes pouring
into heads, like stopped water:
   much seemed
constant, to be looked
forward to, expected:
from the top of a dune rise,
look of ocean salience: in
   the hollow,
where a runlet
   makes in
at full tide and fills a bowl,
extravagance of pink periwinkle
along the grassy edge,
and a blue, bunchy weed, deep blue,
deep into the mind the dark blue
   constant:
minnows left high in the tide-deserted pocket,
   fiddler crabs
bringing up gray pellets of drying sand,
disappearing from air's faster events
at any close approach:
certain things and habits
   recognizable as
having lasted through the night:
though what change in
a day's doing!
desertions of swallows
   that yesterday
ravaged air, bush, reed, attention
in gatherings wide as this neck of dunes:
now, not a sound
or shadow, no trace of memory, no remnant

       explanation:
summations of permanence!
where not a single single thing endures,
the overall reassures,
deaths and flights,
shifts and sudden assaults claiming
limited orders,
the separate particles:
earth brings to grief
much in an hour that sang, leaped, swirled,
yet keeps a round
      quiet turning,
beyond loss or gain,
beyond concern for the separate reach.

First Carolina Said-Song

(as told me by an aunt)

In them days
      they won't hardly no way to know if
        somebody way off
        died
            till they'd be
            dead and buried

        and Uncle Jim

hitched up a team of mules to the wagon
and he cracked the whip over them
        and run them their dead-level best
the whole thirty miles to your great grandma's funeral
          down there in
          Green Sea County

          and there come up this
awfulest rainstorm
        you ever saw in your whole life
        and your grandpa

                    was setting
                    in a goat-skin bottomed chair

        and them mules a-running
        and him sloshing round in that chairful of water

                        till he got scalded
                        he said

                        and ev-
        ery
        anch of skin come off his behind:

        we got there just in time to see her buried
                    in an oak grove up
                    back of the field:

        it's growed over with soapbushes and huckleberries now.

Second Carolina Said-Song

(as told me by a patient, Ward 3-B,
Veterans Hospital, Fayetteville, August 1962)

                    I was walking down by the old
            Santee
                        River
                            one evening, foredark
                            fishing I reckon,

                            when I come on this
            swarm of
            bees
                        lit in the fork of a beech limb
                            and they werz

                            jest a swarming:

                it was too late to go home

and too far
and brang a bee-gum

  so I waited around
  till the sun went
down,
most dark,

  and cut me off a pinebough,
  dipped it in the river
   and sprankled water

on 'em: settled 'em right down,
  good and solid,
about
   a bushel of
  them:

  when it got dark I first cut off
the fork branches and
then cut about four foot back toward
   the trunk

and I
  threwed the limb over my shoulder and
   carried 'em home.

Dunes

Taking root in windy sand
 is not an easy
way
to go about
 finding a place to stay.

A ditchbank or wood's-edge
 has firmer ground.

In a loose world though
 something can be started—

a root touch water,
    a tip break sand—

Mounds from that can rise
    on held mounds,
a gesture of building, keeping,
    a trapping
into shape.

Firm ground is not available ground.

February Beach

Underneath, the dunes
    are solid,
                frozen with rain
        the sand
held and let
go deep
without losing

        till a clearing freeze
left water the keeper of sand:

warm days since
have intervened,
softened

            the surface,
evaporated
the thaw
    and let grains loose: now

the white grains drift against the dunes
and ripple as if in summer,
hiding the hard deep marriage
    of sand and ice:

fog lay thick here
most of the morning

> but now lifting, rides
in low from the sea,
> filters inland through the dunes
but
> over the warm and
sunny sand rising
loses its shape out of sight:

the dense clumps of grass, bent
> over,
still wet with fog,
> drop
> dark buttons of held fog on thin dry sand,
separately, here, there, large drops,
another rainsand shape:

distant, the ocean's breakers
merge into high splintering
> sound,
the wind low, even, inland, wet,
a perfect carriage
> for resolved, continuous striving:

> not the deep breakage and roar
> of collapsing hollows:
> sound that creation may not be complete,
that the land may not have been
given
permanently,
> that something remains
to be agreed on,
a lofty burn of sound, a clamoring and
> coming on:

how will the mix be
> of mound and breaker,
grain and droplet: how
> long can the freeze hold, the wind lie,
the free sand
keep the deep secret: turn: the gold
> grass will come

green in time, the dark stalks of rushes
will settle
    in the hollows, the ice bridge
        dissolving, yielding
will leave solid
bottom for summer fording: the black bushes
      will leaf,
hinder
the sea-bringing wind: turn turn

      here with these chances
taken, here to take these chances: land winds will
rise, feed
back the sands, humble the breakers: today's
      high unrelenting cry will relent:
the waves will lap with broken, separate,
    quiet sounds:
let the thaw that will come, come: the dissolved
      reorganizes
    to resilience.

Moment

He turned and
stood

in the moment's
height,

exhilaration
sucking him up,

shuddering and
lifting

him
jaw and bone

and he said
what

destruction am I
blessed by?

Upright

He said
I am mud
in a universe of stone and fire,

neither hard
enough to last
nor expressed
   in one
of those imperishable fires.

Be something
the grassblade said
rising whitegreen

from common swamp.
I am he
said

nothing &
feel better that
way.

The grassblade
said
be like us

grass stone
and fire and
pass.

Mud is
nothing
and eternal.

Glass

The song
sparrow puts all his
saying
into one
repeated song:
what

variations, subtleties
he manages,
to encompass denser
meanings, I'm
too coarse
to catch: it's

one song, an over-reach
from which
all possibilities,
like filaments,
depend:
killing,

nesting, dying,
sun or cloud,
figure up
and become
song—simple, hard:
removed.

Center

A bird fills up the
streamside bush
with wasteful song,
capsizes waterfall,
mill run, and
superhighway

                    to
                    song's improvident
                    center
                    lost in the green
                    bush green
                    answering bush:
                    wind varies:
                    the noon sun casts
                    mesh refractions
                    on the stream's amber
                    bottom
                    and nothing at all gets,
                    nothing gets
                    caught at all.

Configurations

I

when November stripped
        the shrub,
                what stood
                out
in revealed space was
a nest
        hung
        in essential limbs

2

    how harmless truth
    is
    in cold weather
    to an empty nest

3

dry
leaves

in
the
bowl,
                    like wings

                         4
              summer turned light
              into darkness
              and inside the shadeful
              shrub
                    the secret
                    worked
                    itself into life:

icicles and waterpanes:
recognitions:

                    at the bottom, knowledges
                    and desertions

                         5
speech comes out,
              a bleached form,
nest-like:

                         after the events of silence
                         the flying away
              of silence
              into speech—

                         6
              the nest is held
              off-earth
by sticks;

              so, intelligence
              stays

                out of the ground

erect on a
brittle walk of bones:

                otherwise
                the sea,

            empty of separations

                        7

leaves
like wings
in the Nov
        ember nest:

wonder where the birds are now that were here:
wonder if the hawks missed them:
wonder if
            dry wings
            lie abandoned,
        bodiless
        this
        November:

    leaves—   out of so many
                   a nestful missed the ground

                        8

I am a bush
I am a nest
I am a bird
I am a wind
I am a negg

    I is a bush, nest, bird, wind, negg
    I is a leaf

if I fall what falls:
the leaves fell and the birds flew away and winter came and

9

when
I
am   bringing
singing   those   home
,   two   again
summer   birds
comes
back

10

so what if
lots of
            unfathomable stuff
            remains,
            inconceivable distances,

            closed and open infinities:
so what if
all that, if
            thunderstorms spill the eggs,
            loosen the nest, strew it across
            galaxies of grass and weeds:

who cares what remains when
only the interior
            immaterial
            configuration—

            shape—
            mattered, matters, immaterial, unremaining

11

there is some relationship between
proximity
to the earth and permanence:

        a shrub puts itself into and out of
        the earth at once,

earth and air united by a stem's
polar meshes of roots and branches:

> earth
> shrub
> nest
> leaf
> bird

the bird is somewhere south, unoriented
  to these roots:
the leaves
    though they may not have wandered so far
  are random:

> earth
> shrub
> nest

goodbye, nest, if wind lifts you loose
goodbye, shrub, if ice breaks you down
goodbye,
goodbye

12

the shrub is nothing
    except part of my song:
the bird I never saw is part of my song and
    nothing else:

(the leaves are a great many little notes I lost
    when I was trying to make the song
    that became my silence)

13

the cockbird longs for the henbird
which longs for the nest
    which longs for the shrub which

longs for the earth
which longs for the sun which longs for

14

inside there the woodmeat is saying
                please, please
                        let me put on my leaves
                        let me let the sap go

but the zero bark is saying
                hush, hush
                        the time is not right
                        it's not the right time

the woodmeat is always right
but bark is knowing

Ithaca, N.Y.

When the storm passed,
we listened to rain-leavings,
individual drops in

fields of surprise;
a drop here
in a puddle;

the clear-cracking
drop
against a naked root;

by the window,
the muffled, elm-leaf drop,
reorganizing at the tip,

dropping in another
event to the ground:
we listened and

liveliness broke
out at a thousand quiet
points.

Holding On

The stone in my tread
sings by the strip of woods
but is
unheard by open fields:

surround me then with walls
before I risk
the outer sight, as, walled,
I'll soon long to.

Attention

Down by the bay I
kept in mind
at once
the tips of all the rushleaves
and so
came to know
balance's cost and true:
somewhere though in the whole field
is the one
tip
I will someday lose out of mind
and fall through.

Way to Go

West light flat on trees:
   bird flying

deep out in blue glass:
uncertain wind
stirring the leaves: this is
the world we have:
take it

Reflective

I found a
weed
that had a

mirror in it
and that
mirror

looked in at
a mirror
in

me that
had a
weed in it

Butterflyweed

The butterfly that
named the weed
drank there, Monarch,
scrolled, medallioned—
his wings lifted close
in pale underwing salute

occasionally would
with tense evenness
open down

hinged coffers
lawned against the sun:

anchored in
dream, I could hardly
fall when earth
dropped and looped away.

Street Song

Like an
eddying willow leaf
I stand

on the street
and turn:
people,

both ways coming
and going
around me, swirl:

probably I
am no stiller—
detached; but

gold is
coming
into my veins.

Contingency

Water from the sprinkler
collects
in street-edge gravel and
makes rocky pools: birds
materialize—puff, bathe
and drink: a green-black

grackle lopes, listing,

across the hot street, pecks
a starling, and drinks: a

robin rears misty with
exultation: twittering comes
in bunches of starts and
flights: shadows pour
across cement and lawn: a
turn of the faucet
dries every motion up.

Trap

White, flipping
butterfly,
paperweight,

flutters by and
over shrubs,
meets a binary

mate and they
spin, two orbits
of an

invisible center;
rise
over the roof

and caught on
currents
rise higher

than trees and
higher and up
out of sight,

swifter in
ascent than they
can fly or fall.

Halfway

This October
rain
comes after fall

summer and
drought
and is

a still rain:
it takes leaves
straight

down: the
birches stand
in

pools of them-
selves, the yellow
fallen

leaves reflecting
those on
the tree, that
mirror the ground.

Mays Landing

I sit in sun
light
on a white

yard-bench:
the sparse great
oaks

cower the county
buildings:
a bumblebee

works a head
of marigolds: the
jail back

there, keys rattle
a sheriff
by:

people stand about
in two's and
three's talking,

waiting for
court:
a drunk man

talks loud as
if sobering to
alarm:

an acorn leaps
through leaves and
cracks the ground!

Storm

Branches broken,
the clean meat at the branch knot
turned out white,
traveled by cleared
white light: certain
consequences are

irreversible, arrangements
lost to
death's and black's
scavenging the sweet grain:
well but weakness
went sacrificed to the wind

and the trees, clarified,
compress rootstrength
into remaining flesh
and the leaves that shake
in the aftermath shake
in a safe, tested place.

Landscape with Figures

When I go back of my head
    down the cervical well, roots
        branch
thinning, figuring
    into flesh
and flesh
glimmers with man-old fires
and ghosts
hollowing up into mind
    cry from ancient narrowing
        needle-like caves:

a depth of contact there you'd
    think would hold, the last
        nerve-hair
feeding direct from
    meat's indivisible stuff:
but what we ride on makes us ride
and rootless mind
in a thundering rove
establishes, disposes:
    rocks and clouds
        take their places:

or if place shifts by a sudden breaking
    in of stars
        and mind whirls
where to go
    then like a rabbit it
freezes in grass, order

as rock or star, to let whatever can, come,
pass, pass over: somewhere another human
figure moves or rests, concern
    for (or fear of) whom
      will start and keep us.

Dark Song

Sorrow how high it is
that no wall holds it
back: deep

it is that no dam undermines
it: wide that it
comes on as up a strand

multiple and relentless:
the young that are
beautiful must die; the

old, departing,
can confer
nothing.

World

Breakers at high tide shoot
spray over the jetty boulders
that collects in shallow chips, depressions,

evening the surface to run-off level:
of these possible worlds of held water,
most can't outlast the interim tideless

drought, so are clear, sterile, encased with
salt: one in particular, though, a hole,
providing depth with little surface,

keeps water through the hottest day:
a slime of green algae extends into that
tiny sea, and animals tiny enough to be in a

world there breed and dart and breathe and
die: so we are here in this plant-created oxygen,
drinking this sweet rain, consuming this green.

Spindle

Song is a violence
of icicles and
    windy trees:

rising it catches up
indifferent
    cellophane, loose

leaves, all mobiles
into an organized whirl
    relating scrap

to scrap in a round
fury: violence
    brocades

the rocks with hard silver
of sea water and
    makes the tree

show the power of its
holding on: a
    violence to make
    that can destroy.

Winter Scene

There is now not a single
leaf on the cherry tree:

except when the jay
plummets in, lights, and,

in pure clarity, squalls:
then every branch

quivers and
breaks out in blue leaves.

Anxiety

The sparrowhawk
flies hard to

stand in the
air: something

about direction
lets us loose

into ease
and slow grace.

Sitting Down, Looking Up

A silver jet,
riding the top of tundra clouds,
comes over
maybe from Rio:
the aluminum sun shines
on it
as if it were a natural creature.

Communication

All day—I'm
surprised—the

orange tree, windy, sunny,
has said nothing:
nevertheless,
four ripe oranges have
dropped and several
dozen
given up a ghost of green.

Elegy for a Jet Pilot

The blast skims
over the string
of takeoff lights
and
relinquishing
place and time
lofts to
separation:
the plume, rose
silver, grows
across the
high-lit evening
sky: by this
Mays Landing creek
shot pinecones,
skinned huckleberry
bush, laurel
swaths define
an unbelievably
particular stop.

The Whole Half

In his head
the lost woman,
shriveled,
dry, vestigial,

cried
distantly
as if from
under leaves
or from roots
through the mouths
of old stumps—
cry part his
at her loss,
uneasiness
of something
forgotten
that was nearly pain:
but the man-oak
rising has grown
occupying
a full place
and finding its whole
dome man
looks outward
across the
stream
to the calling
siren tree,
whole—woman.

Belief

for JFK

I

drums gather and humble us beyond escape,
propound the single, falling fact:
time, suspended between memory and present,
hangs unmeasured, empty

2

erect,
disciplined by cadence into direction, the soldier

obeys the forms of rumor:
the riderless horse,
restive with the pressure of held flight,
tosses the hung bit,
worries the soldier's tameless arm—
sidling, prances the energy out

3

ahead, unalterable, the fact proceeds,
and the bit holds:
the fire-needle bites,
training the head on course

4

the light, determined rattle
of the caisson
breaking into sunlight
through the crystal black ribbons of trees!
the slack traces,
weightlessness at the shoulders of horses!

5

if we could break free
and run this knowledge out,
burst this energy of grief
through a hundred countrysides!
if bleak through the black night
we could outrun
this knowledge into a different morning!

6

belief, light as a drumrattle,
touches us and lifts us up to tears.

Mountain Talk

I was going along a dusty highroad
when the mountain
across the way
turned me to its silence:
oh I said how come
I don't know your
massive symmetry and rest:
nevertheless, said the mountain,
would you want
to be
lodged here with
a changeless prospect, risen
to an unalterable view:
so I went on
counting my numberless fingers.

Loss

When the sun
falls behind the sumac
thicket the
wild
yellow daisies
in diffuse evening shade
lose their
rigorous attention
and
half-wild with loss
turn
any way the wind does
and lift their
petals up
to float
off their stems
and go

Zone

I spent the day
differentiating
and wound up
with nothing
whole to keep:

tree came apart from tree,
oak from maple, oak
from oak, leaf from leaf,
mesophyll cell
from cell
and toward dark
I got lost between
cytoplasm's grains
and vacuoles:

the next day began
otherwise: tree
became plant, plant
and animal became
life: life & rock,
matter: that
took up most of
the morning: after
noon, matter began
to pulse, shoot, to
vanish in and out of
energy and

energy's invisible
swirls confused, surpassed
me: from that edge
I turned back,
strict with limitation,
to my world's
bitter acorns
and sweet branch water.

Recovery

All afternoon
the tree shadows, accelerating,
lengthened
till
sunset
shot them black into infinity:
next morning
darkness
returned from the other
infinity and the
shadows caught ground
and through the morning, slowing,
hardened into noon.

Interference

A whirlwind in the fields
lifts sand
into its motions
to show, tight, small,
the way it walks
through a summer day:

better take time to watch
the sand-shadow mist—
since every
grain of sand
is being counted by the sun.

Bay Bank

The red-winged blackbird
lighting
dips deep the

windy bayridge
reed but
sends a song up
reed and wind rise to.

Self-Portrait

In the desert a
clump of rocks
sang with hidden water:

I broke in &
water spilled:
I planted trees:

wild animals from the hills
came at night
to tame water
and stood still:

the air gathered
hoverings of birds
from
drought's celestial trees:

grass sprouted
and spangled into seed:

green reaches of
streams went out:
the rabbit that
had visited,
dwelled:

this was a dream.

Peak

Everything begins at the tip-end, the dying-out,
    of mind:
the dazed eyes set and light
dissolves actual trees:

    the world beyond: tongueless,
unexampled
burns dimension out of shape,
opacity out of stone:

come: though the world ends and cannot
end,
    the apple falls sharp
to the heart starved with time.

Passage

How, through what tube, mechanism,
unreal pass, does
    the past get ahead of us
to become today?

the dead are total mysteries, now:
their radiances,
    unwaxed by flesh, are put out:
disintegrations

occur, the black kingdom separates, loses
way, waters rush,
    gravel pours—
faces loosen, turn, and move:

that fact, that edge to turn around!
senselessly, then,
    celebrant with obscure
causes, unimaginable means, trickles

of possibility, the cull beads
catch centers, round out,
    luminescence stirs,
circulates through dark's depths

and there—all lost still lost—
the wells primed, the springs free,
    tomorrow emerges and
falls back shaped into today.

Laser

An image comes
and the mind's light, confused
as that on surf
or ocean shelves,
gathers up,
parallelizes, focuses
and in a rigid beam illuminates the image:

the head seeks in itself
fragments of left-over light
to cast a new
direction,
any direction,
to strike and fix
a random, contradicting image:

but any found image falls
back to darkness or
the lesser beams splinter and
go out:
the mind tries to
dream of diversity, of mountain
rapids shattered with sound and light,

of wind fracturing brush or
bursting out of order against a mountain
range: but the focused beam

folds all energy in:
the image glares filling all space:
the head falls and
hangs and cannot wake itself.

Kind

I can't understand it
  said the giant redwood
    I have attained height and distant view,
    am easy with time,

  and yet you search the
  wood's edge
for weeds
that find half-dark room in margins
    of stone
    and are
as everybody knows
  here and gone in a season

  O redwood I said in this matter
I may not be able to argue from reason
but preference sends me stooping
seeking
    the least,
    as finished as you
    and with a flower

Money

Five years ago I planted a buttonwood slip:
three years ago I had to fit myself
into its shade, a leg or arm
left over in light:
now I approach casually and
lost in shade more than
twice my height and several times my width

sit down in a chair
and let the sun move through a long doze.

Height

There was a hill once wanted
to become a mountain
        and
forces underground helped it
    lift itself
    into broad view
and noticeable height:

but the green hills around and even
some passable mountains,
        diminished by white,
wanted it down
so the mountain, alone, found
    grandeur taxing and
    turned and turned
to try to be concealed:

oh but after the rock is
massive and high . . !
        how many centuries of rain and
ice, avalanche
and shedding shale
    before the dull mound
can yield to grass!

Fall Creek

It's late September now
and yesterday
finally

after two dry months
the rain came—so quiet,
a crinkling

on
flagstone and leaf,
but lasting:

this morning
when I walked the bridge over
the gorge

that had been soundless
water shot out over rock
and the rain roared

Utensil

How does the pot pray:
wash me, so I gleam?

prays, crack my enamel:
let the rust in.

Mission

The wind went over
me
saying
why are you so distressed:

oh I said I
can't seem to make
anything
round enough to last:

but why
the wind
said
should you be so distressed

as if anything here belonged to you
as if anything here were your concern.

The Fall

I've come down a lot on the tree of terror:
   scorned I used
   to risk the thin bending lofts
     where shaking with stars
I fell asleep, rattled, wakened, and wept:

I've come down a lot from the skinny
   cone-locked lofts
   past the grabbers and tearers
     past the shooing limbs, past the fang-set
eyes

and hate-shocked mouths:
   I rest on sturdier branches and sometimes
   risk a word
     that shakes the tree with laughter or reproof—
am prized for that:

I've come down into the
   odor and warmth
   of others: so much so that I
     sometimes hit the ground and go
off a ways looking, trying out:

if startled, I break for the tree,
   shinny up to safety, the eyes and
   mouths large and hands working to my concern:
     my risks and escapes are occasionally
spoken of, approved: I've come down a lot.

April

Midafternoon
I come
home to the apartment
and find the janitor

looking up and
policeman looking
up (said he'd

go call Bill—has
a ladder)
and all the old
white-haired women

out looking up
at
the raccoon asleep
on the chimney top:

went up the ivy
during the night and
dazed still with
winter sleep can't

tell whether
to come down
or take
up sleep again—

what a blossom!

He Held Radical Light

He held radical light
as music in his skull: music
turned, as
over ridges immanences of evening light
rise, turned
back over the furrows of his brain
into the dark, shuddered,
shot out again
in long swaying swirls of sound:

reality had little weight in his transcendence
so he

had trouble keeping
his feet on the ground, was
terrified by that
and liked himself, and others, mostly
under roofs:
nevertheless, when the
light churned and changed

his head to music, nothing could keep him
off the mountains, his
head back, mouth working,
wrestling to say, to cut loose
from the high, unimaginable hook:
released, hidden from stars, he ate,
burped, said he was like any one
of us: demanded he
was like any one of us.

High & Low

A mountain risen
in me
I said
this implacability
must be met:
so I climbed
the peak:
height shook and
wind leaned
I said what
kind of country is
this anyhow and
rubbled
down the slopes to
small rock
and scattered weed.

Convergence

My sorrows he said
begin so
deep they join only
at extreme, skinny height:
so he climbed

and water fell
smooth, chasms
lifted into ripples
and earth's slow
curve

merged, emerged:
he stood capable
poised
on the peak of
illusion's pyramid.

Medium

What small grace comes must
count hard
and then

belong to the poem that is in need
not to my own redemption
except

as the mirror gives back the dream:
since I'm guilty
any crime

will do
to pour my costly anguish to:
but

payment is exact,
strict and clear: the purchase
never comes

or if so becomes a song
that takes its blessings to itself
and gets away.

Loft

I live in a bodiless loft,
no joists, beams,
or walls:

I huddle high,
arch my back against the stiff
fact of coming down:

my house admits to being
only above the level of most
perception:

I shudder and make do:
I don't look down.

Garden

I have sung
delphiniums
seasonless, seedless
out of debris,

stone-white asters
out of shale:
I've made it this far
turning between made sights

and recognitions:
and now

if everything becomes,
as it could,

naturalized, returned,
I may pick hyacinths
here real and tender
in the ruse.

Countering

The crystal of reason
grows
down
into my loves and
terrors, halts
or muddles
flow,
casting me to
shine or break:

the savage peoples
wood slopes, shore rocks
with figures of dream
who struggle
to save or
have his life:

to keep the
life and
shape, to keep
the sphere, I hide
contours,
progressions between

turning lines,
toward the higher
reason
that contains the war
of shape and loss
at rest.

Levitation

What are you doing
up there
said the ground
that disastrous to seers
and saints
is always around
evening scores, calling down:

I turned
cramped in abstraction's gilded loft
and
tried to think of something beautiful to say:

why
I said failing
I'm investigating the
coming together of things:

the ground
tolerant of such
widened without sound

while I turning
harmed my spine against
the peak's inner visionless ribs—

heels free
neck locked in the upward drift—

and even the ground I think
grew shaky
thinking something might be up there
able to get away.

Virtu

Make a motion
the wind said and
the mountain
strained hard
but

couldn't
even quiver:

so the wind curved and shook the poplars:
a slope
pebble loosened
and struck

down sharp goings:

the mountain
stunned at being
moved nearly
broke with grief

and the wind
whirled up the valley
over the stream

and trees
utterly unlost
in emptiness.

Gain

Last night my mind limped
down the halls of its citadel,
wavered by the lofty columns
as if a loosened door had
let the wind try inside
for what could go:

dreamed of the fine pane-work
of lofty windows it
would not climb to again to see,
of curved attics aflight with
angels it would not
disturb again: felt the
tenancy of its own house,
shuffled to the great door and
looked out into its permanent dwelling.

Poetics

I look for the way
things will turn
out spiralling from a center,
the shape
things will take to come forth in

so that the birch tree white
touched black at branches
will stand out
wind-glittering
totally its apparent self:

I look for the forms
things want to come as

from what black wells of possibility,
how a thing will
unfold:

not the shape on paper—though
that, too—but the
uninterfering means on paper:

not so much looking for the shape
as being available
to any shape that may be
summoning itself
through me
from the self not mine but ours.

The Mark

I hope I'm
not right
where frost
strikes the
butterfly:
in the back
between
the wings.

Concerning the Exclusions of the Object

Today I
looked for myself,

head full of
stars,

cosmic
dust in my teeth,

and small,
lost

as earth in such a
world, I

fell around my
cell's space

and said
I must be here—how

can I get the seeker
home into these jaws:

how
can I expel these roomy stars?

Dominion

I said
Mr. Schafer
did you get up see the comet:

and
he said
Oh no
let it go by, I don't care:

he has leaves to rake
and the
plunger on his washing machine isn't working right:

he's not amused
by ten-million-mile tails
or any million-mile-an-hour
universal swoosh

or
frozen gases
lit by disturbances

across our
solar arcs

Cougar

Deprived like the cougar
into heights

I knew huge
air, rock
burn,

lightning, sun,
ice,

gained

insouciance:

bend, bend
the stream called high:
but I climbed higher

knowing what
takes rock away.

Saying

I went out on
a rustling day
and
lectured the willow:
it nodded profoundly
and held
out many arms:
I held my
arms up and said things:
I spoke up:
I turned into and
from the wind:
I looked all around:
dusk, sunless,
starless, came:
the wind
fell and left us
in the open
still and bent.

Treaties

My great wars close:
ahead, papers,
signatures, the glimmering
in shade of

leaf and raised wine:
orchards, orchards,
vineyards, fields:
spiralling slow time while
the medlar
smarts and glows and
empty nests
come out in the open:
fall rain then stirs
the black creek and
the small leaf slips in.

Lion::Mouse

Cutting off the
offending parts

plucking out

they were so many I
tore the woods
up

with my roaring losses

but kept on
dividing, snipping away,
uprooting and
casting out

till
I scampered
under
a leaf

and considering
my remnant self
squeaked
a keen squeak of joy

Breaks

From silence to silence:
as a woods stream
over a
rock holding on

breaks into clusters of sound
multiple and declaring as
leaves, each one,

filling
the continuum between leaves,

I stand up,
fracturing the equilibrium,
hold on,

my disturbing, skinny speech
declaring
the cosmos.

Locus

Here
it is
the middle of April
(and a day or so more)

and
the small oak
down in
the
hollow is
lit up (winter-burned, ice-gold
leaves on)

at sundown,
ruin transfigured to

stillest shining:
I let it as center
go
and
can't believe
our peripheral
speed.

Admission

The wind high along the headland,
mosquitoes keep low: it's
good to be out:
schools of occurring whitecaps
come into the bay,
leap, and dive:
gulls stroll
long strides down the shore wind:
every tree shudders utterance:
motions—sun, water, wind, light—
intersect, merge: here possibly
from the crest of the right moment
one might break away from the final room.

Heat

The storm built till
    midnight
then full to quietness
broke:
    wind
struck across the surf
hills and
    lightning, sheeting

& snapping, cast
quick shadows, shook
    the rain loose:

this morning
    the flowers on the steep bank
look bedraggled
with blessings.

Cascadilla Falls

I went down by Cascadilla
Falls this
evening, the
stream below the falls,
and picked up a
handsized stone
kidney-shaped, testicular, and

thought all its motions into it,
the 800 mph earth spin,
the 190-million-mile yearly
displacement around the sun,
the overriding
grand
haul

of the galaxy with the 30,000
mph of where
the sun's going:
thought all the interweaving
motions
into myself: dropped

the stone to dead rest:
the stream from other motions
broke
rushing over it:

shelterless,
I turned

to the sky and stood still:
Oh
I do
not know where I am going
that I can live my life
by this single creek.

Definitions

The weed bends
   down and
becomes a bird:
the bird
   flies white

through winter
   storms: I
have got my
interest up in
   leaf

transparencies:
   where I am
going, nothing
of me will remain:
   yet, I'll

drift through the
   voices of
coyotes, drip
into florets by
   a mountain rock.

Path

Leaves are eyes:
light through
translucences
prints
visions that
wander:

I go for a walk and my image
is noticed by the protoplasm:

I wonder what visions
the birch-heart
keeps dark:
I know their cost!
the heart shot
thin that
pays winter hard:

I am run so seen and thin:
I see and shake

Love Song

Like the hills under dusk you
fall away from the light:
you deepen: the green
light darkens
and you are nearly lost:
only so much light as
stars keep
manifests your face:
the total night in
myself raves
for the light along your lips.

Love Song (2)

Rings of birch bark
stand in the woods
still circling the nearly
vanished log: after
we go to pass
through log and star
this white song will
hug us together in the
woods of some lover's head.

The Woodsroad

I stop on
the woodsroad,
listen:
I take myself in:

I let go the locust's
burr-squall, pointless,
high in the pine:
I turn all

the clouds crossing
above me loose:
I drop free of
the fern's sori:

I zoom home through,
as if hailstruck,
caterpillar-pocked
whiteoak leaves:

I take myself
all in, let go &
float free: then
break into

clouds, white dots on
dead stalks, robin
mites: then, I'm here:
I listen: call.

Mediation

The grove kept us dry
subtracting from
the shower much
immediacy:

but then distracted us
for hours, dropping
snaps faint as the twigs
of someone coming.

Crevice

Seeing into myth is
knowledge myth can't sanctify:
separating symbol and
translucence
disembodies belief:
still, nothing's changed:
the slope that
falls here toward the lake
has held
since the first mind figured
in and out of shape:
but a constant in change
no hand or sight has
given definition to:
how are we new from the slow
alterations now:
we stand around dazed
and separate, sunless and eventful:
mind can't charge the slope:
again we've fallen wise.

Snow Whirl

The snow turning
crosshatches the air
into
tilted squares:

I sit and think
where to dwell:

surely, somewhere before,
since snow
began to fall,
the wind has

managed to turn
snow into
squares of emptiness:

dwell there
or with the flakes
on one side of the motion
squareless,

dropping in an
unreturning slant.

Reversal

The mt in my head surpasses you
I said

becomes at the base
more nearly incalculable with

bush
more divisive with suckers and roots

and at the peak
far less visible

plumed and misty
opening from unfinal rock to air:

arrogance arrogance
the mt said

the wind in your days
accounts for this arrogance

This Bright Day

Earth, earth!
day, this bright day
again—once more
showers of dry spruce gold,
the poppy flopped broad open and delicate
from its pod—once more,
all this again: I've had many
days here with these stones and leaves:
like the sky, I've taken on a color
and am still:
the grief of leaves,
summer worms, huge blackant
queens bulging
from weatherboarding, all that
will pass
away from me that I will pass into,
none of the grief
cuts less now than ever—only I
have learned the
sky, the day sky, the blue
obliteration of radiance:
the night sky,
pregnant, lively,
tumultuous, vast—the grief
again in a higher scale

of leaves and poppies:
space, space—
and a grief of things.

Auto Mobile

For the bumps bangs & scratches of
collisive encounters
madam
I through time's ruts and weeds
sought you, metallic, your
stainless steel flivver:
I have banged you, bumped
and scratched, side-swiped,
momocked & begommed you &
your little flivver still
works so well.

Involved

They say last night radiation
storms spilled down the meridians,
cool green tongues of solar
flares, non-human & not
to be humanized, licking at
human life: an arctic
air mass shielded us: had I been
out I'd have said,
knowing them masked, burn me: or
thanks for the show:
my spine would have flared
sympathetic colors:
as it is I slept through,
burning from a distant source.

Project

My subject's
still the wind still
difficult to
present
being invisible:
nevertheless should I
presume it not
I'd be compelled
to say
how the honeysuckle bushlimbs
wave themselves:
difficult
beyond presumption

Impulse

If a rock on the slope
loosens tonight
will it be because
rain's
unearthed another grain
or a root
arched for room
and
will a tree or rock
be right
there, or two rocks or trees,
to hold the
flashed decision back?

Undersea

Foraminiferal millennia
bank and spill but

even so
time's under pressure of
diatomaceous event,
divisions a moment
arcs across:
                    desperate
for an umbrella, net, longpole,
or fan: so much
to keep for paradigm,
so much to lose.

Transfer

When the bee lands the
morning glory bloom
dips some and weaves:
   the coming true of
   weight
   from weightless wing-held
   air
   seems at the touch
   implausible.

Body Politic

   Out for stars he
   took some
   down
   and we all
   wondered if he might be
   damned to such sinister
   & successful enterprise:
   we took and
   unfolded him: he
   turned out
   pliant and warm
   & messy in
   some minor way: then, not

having come to
much, we
lit into his stars which
declaring nothing dark
held white and high
and brought us down.

Offset

Losing information he
rose gaining
view
till at total
loss gain was
extreme:
extreme & invisible:
the eye
seeing nothing
lost its
separation:
self-song
(that is a mere motion)
fanned out
into failing swirls
slowed &
became continuum.

Civics

Hard up for better lays (with
fewer diseases)
a less qualified gliding,
he took
amelioration seriously,
thought the poor deserved better
dreams, that
taxes should husband

unwed mothers, house
the losing mad,
raised money for
churches
& otherwise by rising
and increasing
spent himself so his old
eat-up woman got
little of his coin:
there are a number of possibilities.

Mechanics

A clover blossom's a province:
actually: florets cluster helical
villages with visible streets:
down the main arteries a ways
leaffarms produce common sustenance:
the kingbee when all is ready
visits and tries the yellow-doored
purplish houses for virgin
sweet, feeds in winged spells,
rumples everything, and leaves behind
not as a gift or fee—seed, seed.

The Quince Bush

The flowering quince bush
on the back hedge has been
run through by a morning
glory vine

and this morning three blooms
are open as if for all light,
sound, and motion: their adjustment
to light is

pink, though they reach for
stellar reds and core violets:
they listen as if for racket's
inner silence

and focus, as if to starve, all motion:
patterns of escaped sea
they tip the defeated, hostile,
oceanic wind:

elsewhere young men scratch and fire:
a troubled child shudders to a freeze:
an old man bursts finally and
rattles down

clacking slats: the caterpillar pierced
by a wasp egg blooms inside with
the tender worm: wailing
walls float

luminous with the charge of grief:
a day pours through a morning glory
dayblossom's adequate, poised,
available center.

Reward

He climbed hard,
ledge to ledge, rise,
plateau,
caught his breath,
looked around,
conceived the distances:

climbed on
high, hard: and
made the peak
from which the
major portion of the view was
descent.

Timing

The year's run out
to the tip
blossom on the snapdragon
stalk.

Guitar Recitativos

I

know you love me, baby
know it by the way you carry on around here certain times of the day
      & night
can make the distinction between the willing and the unrefusable
hat's not what I'm talking about
hat's not what I need
Vhat I mean is could you just peel me a few of those grapes over there
want to lie here cool and accumulate . . .
Oh about half a bunch
hat's what I need
            —flick out those little seed—
ust drop 'em in here one at a time
m not going anyplace, baby, not today
elax—sneak the skin off a few of those grapes for me, will you?

2

aby, you been stomping round on my toes so long
hey breaking out in black and blue hyacinths,
Vell-knit forget-me-nots
eraniums are flopping out over the tops of my shoes
ndril leaves coming out along the edges of my shoelaces

ladioli are steering out of the small of my back
  strumming their cool stalks up my spine
innias radiating from the crock of my neck
d petunias swinging down bells from my earlobes
ll this stomping around on me you been doing, baby,

I'm gonna break out in a colorful reaction
I'm gonna wade right through you
    with the thorns of all these big red roses

                        3

I can tell you what I think of your beauty, baby,
You have it, it's keen and fast, there's this
glittery sword whipping about your head all day
and, baby, you make people snap—you condescend

and a surprised little heart splatters or you turn your
cold head away and a tiny freeze kills a few
cells in some man's brain—I mean, baby, you
may be kind but your beauty sweetie is such

many a man would run himself through for
hating your guts every minute that he died for you

                        4

I'm tired of the you-and-me thing
I am for more research into the nature of the amorous bond
the discovery of catalysts for speeding-up, wearing out, and getting it
            over with
or for slowing it down to allow long intervals of looseness

Baby, there are times when the mixture becomes immiscible
and other times we get so stirred up I can't tell
whether I'm you or me
and then I have this fear of a surprising reaction in which
we both turn into something else

powdery or gaseous or slightly metallic
What I mean is this whole relationship is, lacking further
knowledge, risky: while there's still time, why
don't you get yourself together and I'll

get myself together and then we'll sort of shy out
of each other's gravitational field, unstring the
electromagnetism and then sort of just drop this
whole orientation baby

5

You come in and I turn on:
freon purrs and the
refrigerator breaks out with hives of ice
The Westinghouse portable electric fan flushes
   my papers all over the room
The waffle-iron whacks down sizzling imaginary waffles
One paper glues itself and billows to the back of the fan
   my nerves nervous as newspapers

I tell you you are a walking calamity
And when you sit down there is hardly less activity
The alarm clock breaks out raging its held cry
and the oven in the kitchen sets itself for broil
I mean the gas-jet in the incinerator bloops on
and frankly the mechanisms in my legs—I hope you
never find out—jerk:
Oh, beauty, beauty is so disturbingly nice.

Trouble Making Trouble

      The hornet as if
      stung twists
      in the first cold,
      buzzes wings

      that wrench him
      across the ground but
      take on no
      loft or

      direction:
      scrapes with feelers
      his eyes to find
      clearance

      in the crazing
      dim of things, folds
      to bite his tail (or
      sting his

head) to life or
death—hits the
grill of a stormdrain
and drops.

Rome Zoo

Subtract from that shower
each leaf's take
and the oak's
shadow is bright dust:
great
yellow helium
rabbits with bluetipped ears
stick the mist-weight
rain and, from high
tussling, yield
all the way to the ground:
the rhinoceros's back darkens.

Small Song

The reeds give
way to the

wind and give
the wind away

Alternatives

I can tell you what I need is one of those
poles Archimedes, thrust
into an unparalleled transform of intellect to power,
imagined dangling on the end of which he could
move the world with: he was as much a dreamer

as I was (sic): I thought, given
a great height, I could do it with words:
still in a sense I have the dream, I have
Archimedes's dream, that is, it hasn't been tried yet
for sure with a pole: with words, I tried it.

Positions

I can tell you what I need is for
somebody to asseverate I'm a poet
and in an embroilment and warfare of onrushing words
   heightened by opposing views
to maintain I lie down to no man in
the character and thrust of my speech
and that everybody who is neglecting me far
   though it be, indeed, from his mind
is incurring a guilt complex
he'll have to reckon with later on
and suffer over (I am likely to be
recalcitrant with leniency):
what I need I mean is a champion or even
   a host of champions,
a phalanx of enthusiasts, driving a spearhead
or one or two of those big amphibian trucks
through the peopled ocean of my neglect:
I mean I don't want to sound fancy but
what I could use at the moment is
a little destruction perpetrated in my favor.

Reassessing

I can tell you what I need, what I need
is a soft counselor laboriously gentle
his warm dry hands moving with a vanishing persistence
to explain to me how I fell into this backwater,
verse: oh what is the efficacy of
this lowgrade hallucination, this rhythm not even

a scientific sine curve:
I mean I need him to wave it all away,
syllables spilling through the screens of
his soft joints, erasing
in an enchantment similar to that I would evoke
all this primitive tribal hooting
into some wooden or ratty totemic ear:
boy, I need to hear about the systems analysts,
futurists, technocrats, and savvy managers
who square off a percentage of reality and name their price.

Renovating

I can tell you what I need is a good periodontist:
my gums are so sensitive, separated and lumpy,
I have to let my cornflakes sit and wilt:
the niacin leaks out before I get it in
and the ten percent daily requirement of iron
rusts: I've got so mashed potatoes best
accommodate my desire: my gums
before them
relax and, as it were, smile: I have bad dreams that
snap, crackle, and pop (to switch seeds)
have built an invisible wall soggy-resistant: what
I could use with my gum line
is like a new start
or at least a professionally directed reversal or
arrest of what has become abrupt recession.

Devising

I can tell you what I need is
money and I don't mean
a few thousand piddling shares of Standard Oil or
Xerox or a chunk
of some up-and-coming (now over-the-counter) computer or
computer component stock:

what I need is a kind of expansive diversification
with exploding international implications,
pools, banks, and, in a figure, shoals
of residual and seminal coin: what I need
to do is adopt a couple of ministates
and then enforce upon the populace the duty
of eating walnuts (which I'd ship in or
aid in the local growth of) and then
the populace would be free
to do anything else it chose before or after or
even while eating walnuts
and then I'd return the fleet (or
else move myself to a ministate)
to bring the shells back for my fireplace:
I like a nice walnut-shell fire
on a coolish autumn night.

Emplacement

I can tell you what I need is
a stronger assortment of battleboasts:
I mean I need visions of toothy monsters
so old greens rot their sludgy toes
so that meeting such visions (and, indeed,
apparently they cannot be avoided) I could
fetch myself up
on a blood-lilting flinching flight of battleboasts:
for I perceive the great work to be done is
too often mismangled in committee, so lacks
all identity, all measuring out into
salient, songster-mongered cherishing:
what I need is for somebody to first of all
point me out a monster and then
loosen a word-hoard or two jacking
my spine up to the duty for
to tell the truth my imagination's sometimes
as pale as my spine's always yellow.

Touching Down

Body keeps talking under the mind
keeps bringing up lesser views
   keeps insisting
     but coaxingly in pale tones

that the mind come on back, try
to get some rest,
   allow itself to
     be consoled

by slighter rather than slackened
thirst: body keeps with light touch
   though darkening
     lines sketching

images of its mortality but not
to startle the mind further off
   hums
     all right all right

Spring Coming

The caryophyllaceae
like a scroungy
frost are
rising through the lawn:
many-fingered as leggy
   copepods:
a suggestive delicacy,
lacework, like
the scent of wild plum
   thickets:
also the grackles
with their incredible
vertical, horizontal,
reversible

tails have arrived:
such nice machines.

Father

I dreamed my father flicked
in his grave
then like a fish in water
wrestled with the ground
surfaced and wandered:
I could not find him
through woods, roots, mires
in his bad shape: and
when I found him he was
dead again and had to be
re-entered in the ground:
I said to my mother I still
have you: but out of the
dream I know she died
sixteen years before his
first death:
as I become a child again
a longing that will go away
only with my going grows.

Script

The blackbird takes out
from the thicket down there
uphill toward
the house, shoots
through a vacancy in the
elm tree & bolts
over the house:
some circling leaves waving
record
size, direction, and speed.

Ocean City

Island-end here is
elongated as a
porpoise's nose, all
lawns and houses
except one spot
where bending property lines have
turned out odd,
giving this plot
the sanctuary of contention—
bayberry, wild
cherry, plum thicket:
a shore hawk
knows the spot,
knows grackles, sparrows,
cardinals, even
mockingbirds cluster here:
he drops by &
right here in town
some early mornings wilderness
meets wilderness
in a perfect stare.

Round

I sat down
from too much
spinning & spun
the big spin's calm:
I said
this is
like it is:

bluebirds
stripped my shoelaces
for nesting:
pill bugs took the cool

under my shoesoles
and weeds, sprung up,
made me their

windbreak:
I said
this is
like it is
and got up turning
out of the still into
the spinning dance.

Chasm

Put your
self out
and you're
not quite
up to
it or
all in

Mean

Some drippage and spillage in
active situations:
efficiency's detritus,
fall-out from happenstance:
a, probably calculable,
instrank of frabigity:
people accustomed to the wide terrain
know, with little alarm, some
clumps are dissolving:
singular's the terrible view
from which the classy gods
take up glassy lives.

Meteorology

Reality's gossed guzzlings,
bristle-eyed
in light
mare's-tails of bleached
speech have
unmaimed the handshrunk
blessings,
declotted the conveyances:
the bleakies
sung against
sweep soaring (that's
delightful) into
high seed
but come back
heebies and harpies
ever
scratching &
fartching:
confine self to
"extremities & superfices"
the unenterable core's rusty
lode shut up.

Up

A clown kite, my
self rustles
up
to any gust:
warps & whucks
the wind: O
my blustering orange
and striped green
immensities!
I get sometimes so
good
tickled at my

self I slip
flat down and
windless
make no
show of grief.

Bearing Mercy

I spent with her
a
merciful night of
lubes &
loblollies,
of goings out
& in &
by & through:
I held her
in the teeth of my
need:
I turned her round
smartly
like a fumbled
beachball: in
the morning she
got up
& her tiny hand
touched her
hair, day's
first flower.

After Yesterday

After yesterday
afternoon's blue
clouds and white rain
the mockingbird
in the backyard
untied the drops from
leaves and twigs
with a long singing.

Making

In wingbar light
the mockingbird
takes the day into
making
takes the clouds still
shipping stars
takes the spring trees'
black small leaves
and with staid motions
and many threads
brings into
view
lightens
and when morning
shows sings
not a whit more beautifully
because it has been dark.

Tossup

This wall interrupts the wind:
sand falls out:
bushes loft vines
& mockingbird &
caterpillar have their ways:
is this wall anything more than
an interruption:
nothing outlasts the last things
across the surfaces of Nothing:
okay I said
I believe in faith,
this soft determination,
this blasted wall.

Plexus

The knot in my gut's
my good center:
I can trim
off fume & froth,
glob & dollop,
come in there and
be
hard as indivisible:
or trusting
the locked twist
float off office
buildings of glassy
mind,
confident if they
don't land they'll
circle back some day.

Working with Tools

I make a simple assertion
like a nice piece of stone
and you
alert to presence and entrance
man your pick and hammer

and by chip and deflection
distract simplicity
and cut my assertion
back to mangles, little heaps:

well, baby, that's the way
you get along: it's all right,
I understand such
ways of being afraid:
sometimes you want my come-on

hard, something to
take in and be around:

sometimes you want
a vaguer touch: I understand
and won't give assertion up.

Three

The floodcrest of afternoon passes:
the blood smooths:
they say a roar's in the world:
here nothing is loud or incomplete:
the yellow iris with a fabulous surrender
has flopped triple-open, available:
sheaves of pointed fingers,
clusters of new holly leaves assume
the air: the redwinged blackbird's
jeer's aboriginally whole in the
thicket across the street: if nothing's
broken, then I'm alone for sure.

Off

Morning's the woman time of day,
light rising
as in a small failure,
the parting of fog
to cloud,
the casual centerless thunder
and the rain beginning
so sporadic
the eye can hardly weave the evidence
and then rain
deep rain
windless,
the iris unshook from its beads,
the firs like old old
men dripping their bottoms wet:
I catch my breath

I throw my clothes on
I have to get out of the house and,
out, my eyes'
concision shoots to kill.

Circles

I can't decide whether
the backyard stuff's
central or irrelevant:
how matted rank the mint is! and
some of the iris stalks are so
crooked rich
the blossoms can't burst
(scant weeds
pop their flowers fast) loose
and the pansies keep
jointing up another blooming tier:
I can't figure out what
the whole green wish again
is, tips pushing hard into
doing the same, last
year again, the year before:
something nearer than
the pleasure of
circles drives into the next
moment and the next.

Miss

Wonder if
you're gross
consider the cosmic
particle so scant
it can splink all
the way through
Cheops
nicking nothing

Square

The formulation that
saves damns:
consequently (unsavable)
a periphery riffler
I thread the
outskirts of mandate,
near enough
to be knowingly away &
far enough away to
wind and snap through
riddling underbrush.

Needs

I want something suited to my special needs
I want chrome hubcaps, pin-on attachments
and year round use year after year
I want a workhorse with smooth uniform cut,
dozer blade and snow blade & deluxe steering
wheel
I want something to mow, throw snow, tow, and sow with
I want precision reel blades
I want a console-styled dashboard
I want an easy spintype recoil starter
I want combination bevel and spur gears, 14
gauge stamped steel housing and
washable foam element air cleaner
I want a pivoting front axle and extrawide turf tires
I want an inch of foam rubber inside a vinyl
covering
and especially if it's not too much, if I
can deserve it, even if I can't pay for it
I want to mow while riding

Celestial

The most beautiful, haunting
dusk scenes around here, clumps of
tidal-marsh reeds on a highway's edge
with supple dark-green
cedar and tough bayberry and such
full of widges, mean
and manyful, opaque with invisibility:
nature turns so wide it can afford to
spoil an interweaving of scapes or
flashing an Icarus by endanger the minds
of several listening millions whose
creation was superb if not special.

Correction

The burdens of the world
on my back
lighten the world
not a whit while
removing them greatly
decreases my specific
gravity

Mirrorment

Birds are flowers flying
and flowers perched birds.

Coming To

Like a steel drum
cast at sea

my days,
banged and dented
by a found shore of
ineradicable realities,
sandsunk, finally, gaping,
rustsunk in
compass grass

North Jersey

Ninth-circle concrete
bending in
high suasions like
formal reductions of
perfect fears: refineries
oiling the air:
burnt reeds, a chemical
scald: gouged land &
shoved mounds:
and man
burning fast motions along
the steely wreaths,
the steely wreaths.

Exotic

Science outstrips
other modes &
reveals more of
the crux of the matter
than we can calmly
handle

Even

Complexity o'erwhelms the gist,
engravities the grist and grits up

the anflob of the flubile:
hurts:
nabs the numbance, fritters the foamost,
fractures the raptors and
rippling rislings:
finding a nut to fit a
bolt is an undertaking.

Hosts

Secrets are slimber black worms
whose appetites are red:
they ball up with searching periphery:
sometimes they string out, roam
the body in a panic of mismanagement:
it's nice when they slacken
(wads of worthy long fellows) and go
to sleep: often they're
sleepless:
some people have more
than others which
makes a difference.

Help

From the inlet
surf a father
pulls in a crab—
a wonderful machinery
but
not a fish: kicks
it off the line &
up the beach
where three daughters
and two sons take
turns bringing cups
of water
to keep alive, to
watch work, the sanded
& disjeweled.

Windy Trees

You'd be surprised how short the roads
in the air are today:
they twist, drop, burst, and climb:
such roads the sparrows have trouble on:
in fact the only thing flying around
here today's the grackle and he
goes over the brush so low looks as if
he's beating something up from hiding:
it's just like reality,
the very day you can't get out to fly
there's also no place comfortable to sit.

Monday

Windowjarring gusts again
this morning:
the surf slapped back white:
shore cherry bushes
trying to
stay put or get away:
the vague storm's
aroused a weekend of
hypochondria: today
the doctors' offices
froth with all
that tried to stay unruffled.

Transducer

Solar floes
big as continents
plunge rasping
against each other:
the noise

flaring into space,
into thinner & thinner
material means
becomes two million
degrees of heat.

Photosynthesis

The sun's wind
blows the fire
green, sails the
chloroplasts,
lifts banks, bogs,
boughs into flame:
the green ash of
yellow loss.

Making Waves

Some mornings of maximal
frustration—wind,
rain four days old—
your hate waves rise &
slap around the walls:
I float, smile, above the
unadmitted show:
but soon, bobbing, send a few
waves out myself and
the two sets
sloshing against each other
agitate the environment
or coming into beat
raise waves so big we both
get scared and hussle out the
oilslicks of consolation.

Clearing

It's day again, the fourth day,
still overcast and sprinkling:
but the wind's stopped:
the trees and bushes in
profound rest
hold beads:
occasionally a bead drops and a
spur of leaves springs upright:
if the sun breaks out an
amazing number of things will change.

Spinejacking

One of these days I'm gonna leave you, baby:
I know it: I can tell:
my bellyfat shakes and knows:
one of these days I'm gonna just
up and outsy: like that:
my dog knows: he
turns around a lot lately:
I don't know if the parrot knows:
it isn't just lately she started scratching:
you always were a kind of bushy bitch:
one of these days I'm gonna just pack off:
you get to make some new
arrangements, then: you like to change
things around, change this one:
one of these days I'm gonna leave you, baby:
I know it: I can tell:
my bellyfat shakes and knows.

The Account

The difference, finding the
difference: earth, no heavier

with me here, will be no
lighter when I'm gone: sum or
subtraction equals zero: no
change—not to the loss of a
single electron's spin—will
net from my total change:
is that horror or opportunity:
should I spurn earth now with
mind, toss my own indifference
to indifference, invent some
other scale that assents to
temporary weight, make something
substanceless as love earth can't
get to with changeless changing:
will my electrical system noumenally
at the last moment leap free
and, weightless, will it
have any way to deal—or if
there is some thinnest weight,
what will it join with, how
will it neighbor: something finer
than perception, a difference
so opposite to ground it will
have no mass, indifferent to mass.

Holly

The hollybush flowers
small whites (become of
course berries)
four tiny petals
turned
back and four
anthers stuck out:
the pistil low &
honey-high:
wasp-bees (those small
wasps or
bees) come around

with a glee too
fine to hear: when
the wind dies
at dusk, silence,
unaffronted,
puts a robe
slightly thinner
than sight over
all the flowers
so darkness &
the terrible stars
will not hurt them.

Winter Saint

In the summer I live so
close to my neighbor I
can hear him sweat:

all my forced bushes, leafy
and birdy, do not
prevent this:

his drawers wrenched
off his sticky butt
clutch my speech white:

his beery mouth wakes up
under my tongue: his
lawnmower wilts my cereal:

I do not like to hear him
wheeze over difficult weeds:
I don't like his squishy toes:

I'm for ice and shutters
and the miles and miles
winter clears between us.

Hippie Hop

I have no program for
saving this world or scuttling
the next: I know no political,
sexual, racial cures: I make
analogies, my bucketful of
flowers: I give flowers to people
of all policies, sexes, and races
including the vicious, the
uncertain, and the white.

Increment

Applause is a shower
to the watertable of
self regard:
in the downpour
the watertable's irrelevant
but after the shower passes
possibility takes on
an extensive millimeter.

Shore Fog

On the cedars and yews
this morning
big drops
(as of rain)
held by finny hands
(but not rain):
fog kept the night all
night awake
and left this morning
in addition to these
big clarities
a close-worked white drift
too multiple to
prevent some dozing.

Banking

Sometimes I see an
enormous loveliness:
I say help like a
deprived nation:
this loveliness
moves & the motion
starves rivers:
the air where
this motion
moves feels
expensive: I go
out where this
is going by and
come back in narrow
about the nose
with some
wilted plants & all
my old peeled sticks.

Tooling Up

I cut a new thread on it this morning,
smeared a little dab (a small glob) of
pipedope around (for perfect action,
should the opportunity arise or
withdrawal prove premature) and
stuck myself out again: a
formal—possibly too formal—stance,
a willed extension, as if in
expectation of pain:
well but I've done my share: my
mind's at ease: I'm
obviously out, my
intentions are obviously firm.

Wagons

Going west
we finally hit
the sea hills, halted
& went down to
see shells, touch
sand and surf, the
peculiar new conditions,
the anguish perfect
that the sun still
took its gold away:
the waves harmless
unharmable posed
no shapes we could
wrestle to the ground:
turning back like
going down ever
diminishes: we
decided maybe we
would hold but
never turn back
and never go down.

Summer Session

Saliences are humming bee paths
in & out around
here, continuous if
unpredictable: they
hang the air with cotton
candy
and make a neighborhood:

we set out four tomato plants a while
ago: good soil

where a row of winter-used cut wood was
I've been out several times to see
but coming dark hinders me,
forcing faith up which
must
spindly as high walloping
weeds
outlast the night:

earlier came a shower so
skinny
not a coil spring in the glass pond
rang the periphery, for a minute:

walking home from class:
dogs yurping
out from hedge tunnels,
jerking to snazzy, skidding halts,
an outrage about the legs,
hairy explosion with
central, floating teeth:
I hope snitching hairy little
worms
will thread their eyelids and distending close off
the eyeballs of flagrant sight the way
summer closed up the
hedges to fill
us with surprises:

in my yard's more wordage than I
can read:
the jaybird gives a shit:
the earthworm hoe-split bleeds
against a damp black clump:

the problem is
how
to keep shape and flow:

the day's died
& can't be re-made:

in the dusk I can't recover
the goldenbodied fly
that waited on a sunfield leaf:

well I can't recover the light:
in my head—on the
inside frontal wall—the fly waits
and then, as he did, darts upward at an
air-hung companion:

ghosts remain, essences out-skinnying
light: essences
perceiving ghosts skinny skinny
percipients:
reverence, which one cannot
withhold, is
laid on lightly, with terror—as if
one were holding a dandelion back
into the sun:

all these shapes my bones
answer to
are going to go on
consuming, the flowers, venations, vines,
the roots that know their
way,
going to go on taking down and
re-designing, are going to go on
stridently
with bunchers & shears
devouring sundry mud, flesh: but their
own shapes will, as will all shapes, break
but will with all
others
cast design ahead where possible, hold
figuration in the cast seed:
shape & flow:
we must not feel hostile:

the most perfect nothingness affords
the widest play,

the most perfect meaninglessness:
look up at dusk and see
the bead fuzzy-buzzy bug
no darker than mist:
couldn't get along
at all except against infinity:
swallow, bat dine
in a rush—
never know what hit him
nothing hit him sent him to nothing:
but the temporary marvels!—
getting along against. . . .
take it from there:

(to slink and dream with the interior singing
attention of snakes)

prolix as a dream, a stream, sameness
of going
but diverse, colorful, sunlit
glints and glimmerings:
can motion alone then
hold you, strange person:
entertainments of flame and water,
flame in water,
an honorable, ancient flame
removed in high burning: water
no less a metal of interest, subtly
obeying: sit down and be consoled:
the death that reaches toward you has
been spared none:
be enchanted with the shrill hunger
of distant children:
do something:

the boughs ripen:
birds falling out
around here like plums,
rolling around, tilting over, turbulent
somersaults, a wrestling with divinity,
smooth & mostly belly:

the tail's a mean instrument but
feathered
gives poise, as of
contrary knowledges:
the cats frizzling with interest tone
down to pure motion: songs go
such way:
destruction of the world into the
guts: regeneration:
the kill is a restless
matter: but
afterwards the fact's
cool as satiation:

we just had lunch at the picnic table
under the elm: chunks of cantaloupe,
peach slices, blueberries, all cool
colorings in a glass cup: hotdogs &
pepsi:
brilliant replenishment:
icy destructions with the berry
burst, the teeth in a freshet
of cantaloupe juice:
the robin's nest, way out on a pear
limb, nearly
overhangs the table: some
worry, of course, a chirp or two:
distant approaches: above, the yellow
triangles of mouths:

up the stairs you go
up the stairs you go
beddybye &
snoozy snooze
up the stairs you go
ho ho
up the stairs you go

now the lawnmowers of reality are
whirring on the slopes of absent lawns
and sunday is in the world or part

of it: I look across the valley
to the otherside big hills and realize
the whole thing's rolling
tumbling in the smoothest quietest
lunge, our
bristlegreen rockship, our clamorous
house wherein difference bites so
hard hardly
a man will admit the common nickelodean core
where metals twist in
slow drifts of warping
pressure:

nevertheless into raw
space we turn, sun
feeding cosmic drift through,
expelling radiance of cosmic storm,
and we are at an
incredible height going round
something:
in the whole coming and going of man
we may not
get around once:
at certain levels recurrence is not
a bore: we clip an arc:

buttered batter's better bitter:

what do you know:
Western Prong beat Old Dock:
stir up them little wasps and you
have a nest of hornets:

past 2 1
women suffer
unbearably (!)
take bladder irritation: that headachy
backachy feeling:
that burning stitching itching gives them
the weewee's, makes them need

fast relaxing comfort: what women go
through
to make or lose a buck: in those
ample haunches
greased with sheer illumination's light
is a mess of bacterial bloomers: it's
merciful to lust the eye's
small-blind: cultures from average nipples:
knowledge is lovely
but some of it shivers
into the blood stream
and undermines the
requirements of the moment: but
desire spills antiseptic gold celluloid
sheathes o'erall
and pours pellucid lubricants
down the drains of microfloral
habitations:
the clitoris rises above
surmountings, backs off, and
takes a testy peck or so:

we went to the park & John swung on
the swings and swung:
little children, I told my wife,
these little children, some of them
will live to say two thousand forty
maybe forty-five, fifty:
I said think of it by that time
we, you and I, will have been dead
so long
worms yet will scoff at us:
it makes you think
(twice):
what are
a few vaginal weeds in the teeth
compared with the traipsing gluebellies of
candorous maggots: & other worms,
all their noise:
get down, yes:

enwarm to eradication the carnal
longings: which are short:

what, then, is the organization of the
soul: scrambles to the peak,
squirts off, slumps back: the
long & short of it:

ducks were there, spinning, sputtering
in the glass: popcorn, wiener rolls
floating in the circumstance: but do
they do do underwater:
if a scientist, I'd devise
a test
and count the dropping abstractions off:
a glass tank with top
and a careful observer
could keep that duck in there
till he had to: yes, but the
test's wrong: suppose the observed's
disturbed & would much have
preferred
to go out upon the ground & hunker up on
a hunk of grass:
could turn to billets due
formerly:
following a duck around au naturel
though
could wobble a man's weltanschauung:
scientific objectivity puts
radiance on
duckshit even: we used to save
coop chickenshit for choicest
garden plants:
a powerful ingredient that
through the delicacies of floral
transfiguration
makes tasty gravy:

friend of mine, brilliant
linguist, told me

a Southern Gentleman screwed
himself in the
penis
with a squirrel's
pizzle:
puzzling:
got it hung in there's how everybody
found out:
doctor had to cut it loose:

let approved channels then be your
contemplation
so you will not wind up in a fix
or fuxy fox, feel the fire asphaltic:
do
not go in for strange devices:
pins, strangulations or such:
practices that lead gradually away
from picnic tables,
the trivial fluvial fumes of sunday braziers:

I'm not going to
delay my emergence:
I'm going to plop
a polyp:
I'm going to pupate
pussycoon:
I'm going to shoot for the wings:
I can't tell you how many times with
stalled interior I've
watched the spiders hatch & thrive:
I'm going to
get something off my chest—
incubus or poking heartflipper:
I'm 42:
the rank & file has
o'errucked me & cloddled on:
I'm not going
any longer officially
to delay my emergence:
I want the head of the matter to

move out of skinny closure:
I want a pumping, palpable turgidity:
I want the condition to take on flare:
I want manifestation silk-dry:

I told this fellow:
I met him out under a soaking
elm tree:
I said you're needy:
you're so needy something's rotten:
I told him just because you have a
mailbox doesn't mean anybody has
to put anything in it:
it's your epidermal hole, nobody else's:
I was getting so much pleasure out
of soaking under the elm tree I
couldn't get interested in the guy's nasty cavity
and knew without looking I wasn't
going to put anything in there:
too bad about the elms being in dutch:

Archie:
   Summer Session has agreed (somewhat
reluctantly) to split 303 into 2
sections, with one for Baxter. I
haven't been able to reconfirm with Bax
that he does still want a second course
but I've gone ahead as if he did, with
the understanding that *someone* will
teach the plus-23 students and do so
at the same time (8:00) as you.
             Barry

seeing in a green yard a sailboat for sale:
worth a morning:
when you consider life
adds up
to exactly nothing:

one day I'm
going to go
out & conjure

the clouds down:
I'm going to try the cape on:
if they don't
come right down
flubbing their responsive damp bellies over the
ambience
I'm going to strip and shit:

as a writing teacher I tell them
revise the world:
they clip, trim, slice:
they bring it in:
oh no I say you've just put it on
stilts:
they lob, twist, crack:
oh no I say when they bring it in
you've killed it:
reconceive:
they bring in something new:
what's the use, I throw up my hands,
we're already two or three worlds
behind:

down this drain, endless
ingestion, getting
bloated with world: anybody toss
an old memo in: it's squirting
milk into treeping squabs:
burning's going on down
there:
the whole world's a few flakes:
it's sedimentation through seas:
those in the heights need
substantial bottoms: need the
sense
things are leveling off: hate
wide, especially open, disparities:

equilibrium fills holes with hills:

feed in a grocery list, somebody:
feed in how to fix a

telescope on, say, a comet: feed in a
few large pieces of legislation,
couple committee reports, some lab
notes, triptickets, sailing schedules,
the dawns & dusks of planets,
contemplations of squirrels:

somewhere along the line the computer
is going to perpetrate a large announcement:
then we'll know why the
imagination's
winding no scraps up into
windy transfigurations:
in our day
comfort is sunrise at 5:25:

couple systems analysts: bushel of
female ticks, engorged: some dirty
rats:
cutworms:
nightfeeders that dusk arouses:
cubic mile of infestation,
corruption, rust, pus, pus
caterpillars,
snot:
tank of wound weepage:
boxcar of love salt,
fill, siftings, winnowings, dregs,
curds, chips,
aerosols of eagerness, dozen black
widows:
a league of universal ivy stone:
choice:
much testament of need: 400
singing horses, a flask of
wart-juice from the udders of the awry:

families with a lot of living to do:
should get turquoise, shaded coppertone,

or spanish avocado:
features for fun-loving families:

discover for yourselves where
the problems are & amass
alternative strategies:
otherwise it's D–& no pussy:

Archie:
   Thanks very
much. That's a
real pleasure.
           Neil

I scribble, baby, I mean
I breeze on:
every mile a twist, I
should be back:
a smidgen slit of silence lets all
in:
the land's turning tables
greased with the finest silence
money can buy, still, the wind, mine & its,
rattles over the ridges, splits
the cords of wood & gristle:
to a cartographer
part of Pennsylvania's a broken record:
curving grooves & ridges in
visual music:

   day after day the camels of the rain
   bear their gray way by: the ditches
   bend green grass in:
   but then drought enlarges in rapids
   the incidence of rocks:
   but then flood, so salient, though
   with muscle swirls, could
   scrape you across a single
   prominence,
   splitting possibility like a paper shell:
   it is, even after an 8-day rain,

hard to know what to ask for:
a baby robin's been out on the
lawn all day, all day wet and for
many days wet though only one
day out: maybe if it were
dry he could get to a low branch at
least, some force from those fumbling
wings, airier dry:

here are the 18-year-old
seedbeds & the
19-year-old fertilizers:
they have come for a summer session:
knowledge is to be my insemination:
I grant it them as one grants flesh
the large white needle:
what shall I tell those who are
nervous,
too tender for needles, the
splitting of iridescent tendons:
oh I tell them nothing can realize
them, nothing ruin them
like the poundage of pure self:
with my trivia
I'll dispense dignity, a sense of office,
formality they can define themselves against:
the head is my sphere:
I'll look significant as I deal with
mere wires of light, ghosts of
cells, working there.

The Imagined Land

I want a squirrel-foil for my martin pole
I want to perturb some laws of balance
I want to create unnatural conditions
I want to eliminate snakes, rats,
     cats, martens from dread
I want above the sloping foil regions of
     exceptional deliverance

I want my evening air trimmed bug clear
  (pits of bottomless change
  shot through the clarifying ambience)
I want design heightened into
  artificial imbalances of calm
I want a squirrel-foil for my martin pole

The Confirmers

The saints are gathering at the real
places, trying tough skin on sharp
    conscience,
endurance in the hot spots—
searching out to define, come up
against, mouth
the bitterest bit:
you can hear them yelping
down in the dark greeny groves of
    condemnation:
their lips slice back
with jittery suctions, cold
insweeps of conjured grief:
if they, footloose, wham up the
precise damnation,
    consolation
may be no more than us trudging
down from paunchy dinners,
swatting hallelujah arms at
dusk bugs and telling them pure
terror has obviously made them
earnest of mind and of motion lithe.

The Makers

We slung do out of the rosy alligator
and

finding him somewhat flattened
    opened

our kits to engines of more
precise destruction
and set in to settled, intense abuse:

lovers and haters of dragons found
themselves
grievously ready to do a little slicing

back:

it was hilarious, stupendous, and quite painful
until
ritualization so overtook us all

that the only product dropping out from
    slitting & stitching was
pocketbooks pocketbooks pocketbooks
from the colorful land of the

September Drift

Hardly anything flies north these days
(a jay occasionally makes the bleak
decision): the robin, sitting on a high
dead elm limb, looks melancholy with
leisure: he thinks, probably: I wonder
how or of what: small bark-searching

birds drift through the shrubs and trees,
the usual feeding, but in one direction:
I guess I won't go anywhere myself, not
that I don't rustle somewhere deep
and remember ice and wolves: I'll stay
to imagine everything can get back.

Tight

I should have had my macadam
driveway re-sealed this fall but
saved a few bucks & let it
go: now the rain pools
out there and the pools
graduate toward each other
with long necks of lonesome
longing: but there's a sort
of idle rain, like today's,
when the drops, large &

sparse, pop huge bubbles
that cruise around smooth
uneventful country: I sat out
there watching a couple of
hours from the garage and got
rapturous trying to think why
that particular show (not to
mention how) ever got devised:
it makes me wonder which way
the economy should be sent.

The Put-Down Come On

You would think I'd be a specialist in contemporary
literature: novels, short stories, books of poetry,
my friends write many of them: I don't read much
and some drinks are too strong for me: my empty-headed

contemplation is still where the ideas of permanence
and transience fuse in a single body, ice, for example,
or a leaf: green pushes white up the slope: a maple
leaf gets the wobbles in a light wind and comes loose

half-ready: where what has always happened and what
has never happened before seem for an instant reconciled:

that takes up most of my time and keeps me uninformed:
but the slope, after maybe a thousand years, may spill

and the ice have a very different look withdrawing into
the lofts of cold: only a little of that kind of
thinking flashes through: but turning the permanent also
into the transient takes up all the time that's left.

The King of Ice

Now and then the intolerable crooks
down around my temples
and binds—an ice-vice, you could
say, vice-ice—a crown of ice:
kings know how to take matters

casually, so I just sit there cold,
intensely inward, brow bowed,
loneliness universal: I wait:
I'm not going anywhere: I
wait for the thing to slip or for

my attention to fix, somewhere on
the inner glacier, on polar bears
in disconcerting romp: I figure
the intolerable not to be dealt with,
just set aside: I am going to

wait: look at these interesting
stitches in my robes, I say:
I've already settled my affairs of state;
that is, I'll take the cold when it comes,
but I will never believe in ice.

Here & Now

Yes but
it's October and the leaves

are going
fast: rain weighted
them and then
a breeze
sent them in shoals clear across
the street

revealing
especially in the backyard
young maple
branch-tip buds that assume
time as far away as
the other side of the sun

Autumn Song

The large is gone—well, it
was mostly vacant: the big
time,
a past and future scoop,
gone, too,
but it was too
big to move much:
I picked up a wet leaf
today: it
left its shape moist
on the macadam
and there was an earthworm
his arteries
shining in the brilliant light—
it really was brilliant today—and
he
panicked at both ends
with the threat of drying out:
a basic
concern I shared with him
and share with him
for I lifted him with the leaf
and took him to the grass:

I'll bet he knows now
he can be seen through and turn
into a little thong:
I knew it all along though I'm
not in grass
and the leaves that fall
give me no sense of refuge.

The Limit

This left hand
side is
the clear edge of
imposition: the other the
thrusting and breaking to possibility:
in between
a tumbling, folding under,
amounting to downward
progression:
the prisoner is not much enamored of compression:
I wonder if this slight
tumbling, brookish, is a large enough motion
to prevent lodged sticks & harrow beavers:
apparently it
can
reach out broadly across the page in space-hungry gesture:
the events a stick makes
coming down a
brook
scraping the bottom
of the ledge-smooth spill—such
events exist in memory
& possibility as in
a silver radiance: the salience,
in a bodiless arrogance,
must preserve
algal tracings or it
loses further (already scared of loss)
ground for possible self-imaginings:

interwork, interwork, it's interwork
that pays with mind because mind
(if an entelechy)—
   shifting over here
   will suggest a tone-gap, slant,
   a redshift as of direction

Looking Over the Acreage

I wonder what I should do now:
probably
I should wait
for the onset or oncoming of a large order,
an aqueduct perhaps
with an endless (theoretically) echo of arches
but which a valley would
break into individual aqueductal shape:
or perhaps an abecedarian procedure
though there are some
problems there
(not everyone is agreed on
what is what)
or I could riffle through the zodiac:
then there are
triads, pentads, dodecahedra,
earth-water-air-fire,
the loft
from indivisibility to all-is-one
(which is where nothing is anything):
descents are less usual
having associations of undesirability
(cities, societies are
exclusive):
the great advantage of an overall arbitrary
order is that one
need not wait until he has earned an order
but may go ahead with some serenity arch
by arch
content if minor forms appear:

one may do that:
I don't know what to do:
no matter what I think I'm probably going to wind up
in both wings of another balance:
    fabulous, ex
cit
ing, over
populated
Hong Kong: yeah.

Spiel

    I feel sure you will be pleased
with our product: it is
a coil spring comes wintrily into
    as house plants
react first to the longer light:

                    but begin all
enterprise with celebration: measures
on the sand by
fluttering rush, sail, heart spun in
a resonance between
departure, grief and adventure of
    change, the hurry and detail,
sudden calamity
of shoving off, moorless into a hunk of
time that may
round back to greet its other edge:
may:

(nothing is so phony as an incomplete
obscurity—it needs spelling
into its deepest outing,
surrounding into its biggest bulging:
when it gets aglitter
it grows black: what to make of a
hinted thing

where the mind's not traveled
but a botch: but spelled out any
spiel can pick enough surfage up
to drum a sea loose)

I just ate a green banana: it is in
me now mushed and gushy: there is
nothing small enough to conjure clarity with:

take the bathroom spider wintered thin:
so thin
bleached out against walls
life seems in him a brown taint that
lacking might make him water or crisp:
he spun an open-ended house
(safety, closed up to perfection,
      traps, he knows)
                  in the ceilingwall sharp
angle:

      (well then I will take a mere
suasion!
a drift
as of earth into light, the chorus
dancing to the right,
left, a multimedial parlance:
well I will take just the angle
the waves come out of the sea, say,
the way they break down their length
in a continuous moving roar:
      I don't care how many drops of
water there are
or how totally they are water or how
the ocean is nothing (figuratively
speaking) else: I identify waves,
they have an
action, many actions: I've seen them
come straight in, crest first in
the middle, break outward both ways
and leave behind

a pyramid of foam: I've never
seen a drop of water do that:)

at night he rides down to the white
sink
and hums in a drop of water's
uptight edge: I try to think
of what he eats
so winter skinny, such a bugless
winter: maybe those tiny book lice
leave learning
scoot ceilings sometimes and suffer
the usual
confrontation with reality:
or I think dandruff scales soaked in
droplets
drift dripping proteins loose that
drunk skirl spiders into hallelujahs
    of darkening:

from the state of distress a pill can
remove you: meanwhile the blue
spruce
is perilously unaffected:

                              it's monsterless here:
the
bayberry in a green sweep, breeze
lively:
indifferent as lace:

swipes, swatches, smears, luminous
samplers: what is

the existence in the argument of what
the argument
is about: precise but unspecified,
hunted out, turned from, disguised,
brunted:

          order, strict,

            is the shadow of flight:
I mean because of the lusterless
structure
the wing has rein: fact
is the port of
extreme navigation:

where footprints
disappear at the edge of melting snow
hesitation breaks mindfully into itself:

      the fairgrounds

(hill meadows, aslant
triangular sweepclosings of heights,
scrub fringes, yangs of woods,
lovely sumac and sassafras, golden
clumps of grass
rising to a wind line, commas,
the pheasant's tail, long,
perfect for disappearance in
winter weeds, clumpy printwork
of rabbits
over hedge-kept floats of snow . . .

I don't know what all there is
but there's more than plenty and
that's just it there's too much
except for, there'd be too much
except for the outgrowth of soothing
hills)

      sporting goods

nip and tuck

scoops
scopes
scrimps &
scroungings

Snow Log

Especially the fallen tree
the snow picks
out in the woods to show:

the snow means nothing by that,
no special emphasis: actually
snow picks nothing out:

but was it a failure, is it,
snow's responsible for
that the brittle upright black

shrubs and small trees
set off what caught the snow
in special light:

or there's some intention
behind the snow snow's too shallow
to reckon with: I take it on myself:

especially the fallen tree
the snow picks
out in the woods to show.

Play

Nothing's going to become of anyone
except death:
    therefore: it's okay
to yearn
too high:
the grave accommodates
swell rambunctiousness &

ruin's not
compromised by magnificence:

that cut-off point
liberates us to the

common disaster: so
   pick a perch—
apple branch for example in bloom—
tune up
and

drill imagination right through necessity:
it's all right:
it's been taken care of:

is allowed, considering

Classic

I sat by a stream in a
perfect—except for willows—
emptiness
and the mountain that
was around,

scraggly with brush &
rock
said
I see you're scribbling again:

accustomed to mountains,
their cumbersome intrusions,
I said

well, yes, but in a fashion very
like the water here
uncapturable and vanishing:

but that
said the mountain does not
excuse the stance
or diction

and next if you're not careful
you'll be

arriving at ways
water survives its motions.

Clarity

After the event the rockslide
realized,
in a still diversity of completion,
grain and fissure,
declivity
&
force of upheaval,
whether rain slippage,
ice crawl, root
explosion or
stream erosive undercut:

well I said it is a pity:
one swath of sight will never
be the same: nonetheless,
this
shambles has
relieved a bind, a taut of twist,
revealing streaks &
scores of knowledge
now obvious and quiet.

Periphery

One day I complained about the periphery
that it was thickets hard to get around in
        or get around for
an older man: it's like keeping charts

of symptoms, every reality a symptom
where the ailment's not nailed down:
        much knowledge, precise enough,
but so multiple it says this man is alive

or isn't: it's like all of a body answering
all of pharmacopoeia, a too
   adequate relationship:
so I complained and said maybe I'd brush

deeper and see what was pushing all this
periphery, so difficult to make any sense
   out of, out:
with me, decision brings its own

hesitation: a symptom, no doubt, but open
and meaningless enough without paradigm:
   but hesitation
can be all right, too: I came on a spruce

thicket full of elk, gushy snow-weed,
nine species of lichen, four pure white
   rocks and
several swatches of verbena near bloom.

Peracute Lucidity

A perspicuity like a sanctuary: against
the pond a pavilion, led to by a glide
of stairs, set right and accurately

gauged: the bobolink in the dusk bush
says a closing say-so: *bunk*
bunk the frog maintains and aims his

tilty eyes: just above the brookfall's
shaggy seams and rags, clarity's chapel
bodied by hung-in boughs: and

widening out over the pond, the blown
cathedral luminous with evening glass:
I go out there and sit

till difference and event yield to
perfect composure: then the stars
come out and question every sound, the brook's.

Working Still

I can't think of a thing to uphold:
the carborundum plant snows
sift-scum on the slick, outgoing river
and along the avenues car wheels

float in a small powder: my made-up
mind idles like a pyramid: oxides
"under proper atmospheric conditions" become
acids and rain a fine broad bleaching:

man's a plant parasite: so I drop
down to the exchange, $CO_2 \leftrightarrow O_2$, and
find dread there, just dread: too
much care fuddles me dull:

beef hormones bloom monstrous
with tenderness:
but I won't take up the scaring cause
and can't think of a thing to uphold.

Upland

Certain presuppositions are altered
by height: the inversion to
sky-well a peak
in a desert makes: the welling

from clouds down the boulder fountains:
it is always a
surprise out west there—
the blue ranges loose and aglide

with heat and then come close
on slopes leaning up into green:
a number of other phenomena might
be summoned—

take the Alleghenies for example,
some quality in the air
of summit stones lying free and loose
out among the shrub trees: every

exigency seems prepared for that might
roll, bound, or give flight
to stone: that is, the stones are
prepared: they are round and ready.

Doubling the Nerve

In the bleak time look for no cooperation
from the birds: crows show up, black blatant
clarions in the gawky branches, to dominate
the rain's dark: grackles on sprung hinges
grate from tree to tree, around:
                                remember
the redbird then in the floral plum, the
bluebird nesting in the apple bough:
remember the white streak in the woodpecker's
wings against shadblow:
                              expect abundance
to yield nothing to privation, no easing
off by contrary song: the quiet world, so
quiet, needs to cut its definitions wide
so snow can rinse across the hard lake.

Ship

Nobody comes here to stay: that's
incredible: and nothing to stay:
the bird tilts tail-up in the high
branch and tilts time away:
well, I don't want to think about that:
the phony comfort about timelessness
time is supposed to work back

into: I've seen no sign of that:
nothing on the re-make or comeback: the
crest breaks, whatever side the sea's on:
the crest bears in and out in a single
motion, not a single point unmoving:
men and women in your loveliness, I cry
nothing against the wall forever giving in.

Early Morning in Early April

The mist rain this morning made glass,
a glittery preponderance, hung baubles
spangled to birch-twig jewelry,

and made the lawn support, item by
item, the air's weight, a lesson as a
various instruction with a theme: and

how odd, the maple branches underlaced
with glaring beadwork: what to make of it:
what to make of a mist whose characteristic

is a fine manyness coming dull in a wide
oneness: what to make of the glass
erasures, glass: the yew's partly lost.

Then One

When the circumstance takes
on a salience, as a

crushing pressure, then one,
addled by the possible closures,

the tangles that might
snap taut in a loop

or other unfigurable construct,
then one

pores on drift-logs far at sea
where room can wear drifts out

winds change
and few places show one can't

embark
from and then one thinks finally

with tight appreciation
of nothingness

or if not that far of
things that loosen or come apart.

Medicine for Tight Spots

Consider big-city
tensions
rurally unwound,

high-tension lines that
loft through the countryside,
give off

"wirelings"
and fine-up to houses
cool as a single volt:

there are so many ways to approach the problems:
reproach:
best of all the by-pass and set-aside: the

intelligence has never been called for
because as usually
manifested it's

too formulated to swim
unformulable reality's
fall-out insistences:

just think how woodsy roads
shade spangled
wind up big-city printed circuits:

if the mind becomes what it sees or
makes how it works
I know which way I'm headed:

won't bushes bust us
mild:
won't the streams

ravel us loose:
won't we be untold
by sweetwater tongues.

Village, Town, City—Highway, Road, Path

Grove, forest, jungle—a thickening motion
accompanied by a sense of loss of control:

swamp: ah, an uncertain or sloppy (hungry) bottom:
flood moccasins lining the bayous, drowning snakes

rafting down the gulf-wide river: patch, copse,
thicket—a surrounding tameness with a touch of

central wilderness: let a dog belch up worms—
they string from his mouth in a white beard,

his eyes grave, tamed, shamed to affliction:
but affliction can storm from shame and

tussle the peripheries of order: but take a word,
there are backward suasions: you may have twice

as much of anything as you ask: my yard maple's
in the open, full of leaf, and single to the wind.

Lonely Splendor

I tell the maple it's unwise—though
it stands open
and alone—to put too much splendor
of leaf on
so that rather than stand firm and quiver
to the wind it rolls
raising whole branches on a swell
that plays out into tossing and twisting
at the top:
but, of course, it is
difficult to tell
the inner thrust it can't ornament the whole
open universe, such quenchless
putting out and on:
I tell the maple, if a wind's taken by
the bounty of your heavy ship,
what may be assumed, what saved:

if I were a maple I'd want neighbors
to keep me skinny and high
in windbreaking thickets:

but then loneliness can't be cajoled
to give a leaf up
(or keep one in)
and can't believe slim thickets
do any slender speaking worthy note.

Life in the Boondocks

Untouched grandeur in the hinterlands:
large-lobed ladies laughing in brook
water, a clear, scrubbed ruddiness lofted

to cones and conifers: frost blurs
the morning elk there and squirrels
chitter with the dawn, numb seed: clarity,

the eagle dips into scary nothingness,
off a bluff over canyon heights: trout
plunder their way up, thrashing the shallows

white: ladies come out in the gold-true sun
and loll easy as white boulders
in the immediate radiance by wind-chilling

streams: I have been there so
often, so often and held the women, squeezed,
tickled, nuzzled their rose-paint luxury:

so many afternoons listened to the rocky
drone of bees over spring-water weed-bloom,
snow-water violets, and distant moss turf.

Brooks & Other Notions

Currents figure
you can see them
they boil out
of themselves &
slice in
from both
sides
a downward crease steady at
the moving burial:

in the wind too
you can feel them
spell
themselves along the
arm, watch them
against an elm

or
multiple on puddles:

below speech
mind
figures motion,
plunges or takes
a turn: grief's
a common
form of going:
its letters rise &
spiel away expressly
inexact.

Hope's Okay

The undergrowth's a conveyance of butterflies
(flusters of clustering) so buoyant and delightful,
filling into a floating impression, diversity's
diversion breaking out into under-piny seas
point by point to the mind's nodes and needs:

let's see, though, said the fire through the undergrowth,
what all this makes into, what difference can
survive it: so I waded through the puffy disgust
and could not help feeling despair of
many a gray, smoke-worming twig, scaly as if alive:

much that was here I said is lost and if I stoop
to ask bright thoughts of roots
do not think I ask for better than was here
or that hope with me rises one leaf higher than
the former growth (higher to an ashless fire) or
that despair came any closer than ash to being total.

The Swan Ritual

Yield to the tantalizing mechanism:
fall, trusting and centered as a

drive, following into the poem:
line by line pile entanglements on,
arrive willfully in the deepest

fix: then, the thing done, turn
round in the mazy terror and
question, outsmart the mechanism:
find the glide over-reaching or
dismissing—halter it into

a going concern so the wing
muscles at the neck's base work
urgency's compression and
openness breaks out lofting
you beyond all binds and terminals.

He Said

Speaking to mountains (&
hearing them speak!) assiduously
(though encounteringly)
avoids the personal,

a curvature whose swerve, however,
can out-range the scary planets

and seriously attenuate
the gravitational
core which wanting the personal
had to give it up:

being can't always be as it is:
volcanoes, droughts, quakes,
natural disasters of all kinds,
including (heavy rain &)

the personal,
mitigate much fixity, the dwelling

of mind in its dwelling:

my immediate sympathetic reaction was
that I understood all that
well in a way

and said it seemed reasonable that
mountains, though,
should attract such voices and
furnish such replies.

The Run-Through

You're sick:
you're on your back:
it's hot:
they take off a leg:
you wake up and feel,
both hands:
you develop pride
in the sewmanship
and show it:

a tube in your skull bursts:
you bleed half
still:
with one arm
you show how
the other flops:
you show, show:
speechless with pantomime:

you're on your back:
it's hot:
they take the other one off:
then you fail
some

with the difficulty
of redundancy:

you're on your back:
you are heavy and hard:
your heart bursts and you are weightless:
you ride to a high stillness:
in death's cure, you exit right.

Runoff

By the highway the stream downslope
could hardly clear itself
through rubbish and slime but by

that resistance gained a cutting
depth equal to its breadth
and so had means to muscle into

ripples and spill over angled
shelves:
and so went on down in a long

curve, responsively slow to the
sizable ridge it
tended

and farther on down, quiet and clear,
never tipping enough to break sound,
slowed into marshy landrise and burst

into a bog of lupine and mirrored:
that was a place! what a place!
the soggy small marsh, nutgrass and swordweed!

The Unifying Principle

Ramshackles, archipelagoes, loose constellations
are less fierce, subsidiary centers, with the
attenuations of interstices, roughing the salience,

jarring the outbreak of too insistent commonalty:
a board, for example, not surrendering the rectitude
of its corners, the island of the oaks an

admonishment to pines, underfigurings (as of the Bear)
that take identity on: this motion is against
the grinding oneness of seas, hallows distinction

into the specific: but less lovely, too, for how
is the mass to be amassed, by what sanction
neighbor touch neighbor, island bear resemblance,

how are distinction's hard lines to be dissolved
(and preserved): what may all the people turn to,
the old letters, the shaped, characteristic peak

generations of minds have deflected and kept:
a particular tread that sometimes unweaves, taking
more shape on, into dance: much must be

tolerated as out of timbre, out of step, as being not
in its time or mood (the hiatus of the unconcerned)
and much room provided for the wretched to find caves

to ponder way off in: what then can lift the people
and only when they choose to rise or what can make
them want to rise, though business prevents: the

unifying principle will be a
phrase shared, an old cedar long known, general
wind-shapes in a usual sand: those objects single,

single enough to be uninterfering, multiple by
the piling on of shared sight, touch, saying:
when it's found the people live the small wraths of ease.

Cut the Grass

The wonderful workings of the world: wonderful,
wonderful: I'm surprised half the time:
ground up fine, I puff if a pebble stirs:

I'm nervous: my morality's intricate: if
a squash blossom dies, I feel withered as a stained
zucchini and blame my nature: and

when grassblades flop to the little red-ant
queens burring around trying to get aloft, I blame
my not keeping the grass short, stubble

firm: well, I learn a lot of useless stuff, meant
to be ignored: like when the sun sinking in the
west glares a plane invisible, I think how much

revelation concealment necessitates: and then I
think of the ocean, multiple to a blinding
oneness and realize that only total expression

expresses hiding: I'll have to say everything
to take on the roundness and withdrawal of the deep dark:
less than total is a bucketful of radiant toys.

Further On

Up this high and far north
it's shale and woodsless snow:
small willows and alder brush

mark out melt streams on the
opposite slope and the wind talks
as much as it can before freeze

takes the gleeful, glimmering
tongues away: whips and sticks
will scream and screech then

all winter over the deaf heights,
the wind lifting its saying out
to the essential yell of the

lost and gone: it's summer now:
elk graze the high meadows:
marshgrass heads high as a moose's

ears: lichen, a wintery weed,
fills out for the brittle sleep:
waterbirds plunder the shallows.

Pluralist

Winds light & variable break
upward out
of cones or drop cones down
that turn up
umbrellalike from the
ground

and even the maple tree's large
enough to express contrary
notions
one side going west & the
other east or northeast or one
up & the other
down: multiple angling:

the nodding, twisting, the
stepping out & back
is like being of two minds
at least
and with the comforting
(though scary) exemplum
that maple trees
go nowhere at all

If Anything Will Level with You Water Will

Streams shed out of mountains in a white rust
(such the abomination of height)
slow then into upland basins or high marsh

and slowing drop loose composed figurations
on big river bottoms
or give the first upward turn from plains:

that's for modern streams: if sediment's
lithified it
may have to be considered ancient, the result of

a pressing, perhaps lengthy, induration:
old streams from which the water's
vanished are interesting, I mean that

kind of tale,
water, like spirit, jostling hard stuff around
to make speech into one of its realest expressions:

water certainly is interesting (as is spirit) and
small rock, a glacial silt, just as much so:
but most pleasurable (magma & migma) is

rock itself in a bound slurp or spill
or overthrust into very recent times:
there waterlike stone, those heated seekings &

goings, cools to exact concentration, I
mean the telling's unmediated:
the present allows the reading of much

old material: but none of it need be read:
it says itself (and
said itself) so to speak perfectly in itself.

Conserving the Magnitude of Uselessness

Spits of glitter in lowgrade ore,
precious stones too poorly surrounded for harvest,
to all things not worth the work
of having,

brush oak on a sharp slope, for example,
the balk tonnage of woods-lodged boulders,
the irreparable desert,
drowned river mouths, lost shores where

the winged and light-footed go,
take creosote bush that possesses
ground nothing else will have,
to all things and for all things

crusty or billowy with indifference,
for example, incalculable, irremovable water
or fluvio-glacial deposits
larch or dwarf aspen in the least breeze sometimes shiver in—

suddenly the salvation of waste betides,
the peerlessly unsettled seas that shape the continents,
take the gales wasting and in waste over
Antarctica and the sundry high shoals of ice,

for the inexcusable (the worthless abundant) the
merely tiresome, the obviously unimprovable,
to these and for these and for their undiminishment
the poets will yelp and hoot forever

probably,
rank as weeds themselves and just as abandoned:
nothing useful is of lasting value:
dry wind only is still talking among the oldest stones.

One More Time

I took my likely schizophrenia in hand
and said if
it must be the high places, let's go to them,
muse how they lie about, see how

the lessening to immateriality occurs,
how the peaks, chipping off, folding in, loft
free to the danger of floating, endure
the falling away, the unneighboring to high isolation:

the essential reductions to form
and to rock, the single substance,
gained, we'll confront puzzling air, from
the strictest consideration to the freest,

and the height made we'll have the choiceless ease
of the single choice, down, and leisure to come on
deepening multiplicity,
trifling, discrete abundance,

bottomless diversity, down into the pines,
morning glories and trout streams
(where the lacewing works the evening, marginal air)
blueberry brush: high-slope cucumber vines abearing.

Transaction

I attended the burial of all my rosy feelings:
I performed the rites, simple and decisive:
the long box took the spilling of gray ground in
with little evidence of note: I traded slow

work for the usual grief: the services were private:
there was little cause for show, though no cause not
to show: it went indifferently, with an appropriate
gravity and lack of noise: the ceremonies of the self

seem always to occur at a distance from the ruins of men
where there is nothing really much to expect, no arms,
no embraces: the day was all right: certain occasions
outweigh the weather: the woods just to the left

were average woods: well, I turned around finally from
the process, the surface smoothed into a kind of seal,
and tried to notice what might be thought to remain:
everything was there, the sun, the breeze, the woods

(as I said), the little mound of troublesome tufts of
grass: but the trees were upright shadows, the breeze
was as against a shade, the woods stirred gray
as deep water: I looked around for what was left,

the tools, and took them up and went away, leaving
all my treasures where they might never again disturb
me, increase or craze: decision quietens:
shadows are bodiless shapes, yet they have a song.

Drought

Bees turn in a fire
of dry-rich honey,
visit the faucet
for the left, crescent
drop: below the faucet
by the cool cement a

webbed bumblebee spins:
the spider, whilom serene,
attacks to feed
another filament in: I
can't understand
for a minute why

the bumblebee
works so hard into the
straitening maze:

but Lord I know why:
it's to find if not flight
the far end of the dark.

Image

The indefinable idol's invisible to the mind:
its visage unmonstrous and unsaintly's unavailable
to the iconoclast who in the whirling wind learns
something of his whirling subduing, which is

primary instruction: of course, it breaks down
into griffins, calves, beavers, gargoyles but
re-summed shoulders up again and disappears: because
it disappears, the put-down's universal and complete:

but then the ignorant and stupid, the unerring
majority, think something's died and promote the
precision of the visibly defined: the more partial,
the more certain, until partiality collapses under

its exclusions: that's another kind of death
that draws human blood: oh, how I wish the notion
of unity could get around: how I wish the idol could
hold summed his attributes, empty free the mind.

Equinox

I went out to cut a last batch of zinnias this
morning from the back fencerow and got my shanks
chilled for sure: furrowy dark gray clouds with
separating fringes of blue sky-grass: and dew

beaded up heavier than the left-overs of rain:
in the zinnias, in each of two, a bumblebee
stirring in slow-motion, trying to unwind
the webbed drug of cold, buzzing occasionally but

with a dry rattle: bees die with the burnt honey
at their mouths, at least: the fact's established:
it is not summer now and the simmering buzz is out of
heat: the zucchini blossoms falling show squash

overgreen with stunted growth: the snapdragons have
suckered down into a blossom or so: we passed
into dark last week the even mark of day and night
and what we hoped would stay we yield to change.

Russet Gold

The shoddy furbishings I pick and choose among,
having, as I have, little hope of the foil brights
shimmering, those ghastly ecstatic blankouts

of rosy coordination in complete deliveries: no:
I take the radiance in, for example, rain, or shiver
to drops beaded up on cellophane: I tell you

when the bark loosens on a soggy stick, I can
get into that space and respire: and have thoughts
otherwise difficult, if not impossible, to assume:

half the time I'm unable, frankly, from a hurtful
capacity to imagine my own privation: but the other
half, I can wait with a yew drop, whether it will

evaporate or, struck by a rapid augmentation, splish,
presuming that the rain is, as here it often is, light
if long: when everything's given up,

amazingly, I think, so much stuff to give up,
and reluctantly, appears: everybody's seen a cast
feather, the dislocation: that's something: and when

a zinnia turns all cone, it's certainly not into
disorder or waste: I don't expect to busy
much with or in the sun, ghosts my valid glimmerers.

Essay on Poetics

Take in a lyric information
totally processed, interpenetrated into
wholeness where

a bit is a bit, a string a string, a
cluster a cluster, everything beefing up
and verging out

for that point in the periphery where
salience bends into curve
and all saliences bend to the same angle of

curve and curve becomes curve, one curve, the whole curve:
that is information actual
at every point

but taking on itself at every point
the emanation of curvature, of meaning, all
the way into the high

recognition of wholeness, that synthesis,
feeling, aroused, controlled, and released:
but then find the wholeness

unbelievable because it permits
another wholeness,
another lyric, the same in structure,

in mechanism of existence, but bearing a different weight,
that is, a different, perhaps contradicting,
bit-nature and assimilation:

wholeness then is a condition of existence,
a one:many mechanism, internally irrelevant to scope,
but from the outside circumscribed into scope:

I like the order that allows, say, when
a thousand cows are on a thousand acres,
clusters to flow out in single file down a gully,

circlings of drinkholes, concentrations in a green
ottom, spread-outs, but identifiable, across
broad rise or scape: I like that just as I

ke tracings converging into major paths,
ntracings of widening out beyond a clump of
ees or small pass:

ose configurations, rendered by aerial photography,
ould interest me endlessly
the precision of their topographical relations:

e interests of cows and the possibilities of
e landscape could be read (not a single actual cow)
ere well: and nothing be as a consequence known and

et everything in a sense known, the widest paths
e controlling symbols, with lesser resemblances of
otion: after a while I could account for the motions of

e whole herd and make interesting statements:
r example, with experience, I bet I could tell
om the wear under a copse

hether a lot of hot sunny days in a year
r windy days come: I could tell something obvious already
om the copse whether it constitutes a meaningful

indbreak in a cold wind, sand or snow storm, and then
at, though obvious, would tell about cows:
l bet in warm climates with heavy, maybe daily, rains

ere'd be little wear under trees, for the cows
ould enjoy being out in the showers:
nyway, there's a time when loose speech has to give in,

me up to the corral, run through the planked alleys,
cept the brand, the medication, surrender to the
entity of age, sex, weight, and bear its relationship

the market: there's no market for most speech, specially
od, and none for loose: that's why I don't care
w far I wander off;

I wouldn't care if I found a whole year gone by and myself
not called for: the way I think is
I think what I see: the designs are there: I use

words to draw them out—also because I can't
draw at all: I don't think: I see: and I see
the motions of cowpaths

over a non-existent, thousand-acre ranch: (times
frequently recur in good scope in which I don't see):
stop on any word and language gives way:

the blades of reason, unlightened by motion, sink in,
melting through, and reality's cold murky waters
accept the failure: for language heightens by dismissing reality,

the sheet of ice a salience controlling, like a symbol,
level of abstraction, that has a hold on reality and suppresses
it, though formed from it and supported by it:

motion and artificiality (the impositional remove from reality)
sustain language: nevertheless, language must
not violate the bit, event, percept,

fact—the concrete—otherwise the separation that means
the death of language shows: when that happens abandonment
is the only terrible health and a return to bits, re-trials

of lofty configurations: if the organism of the ranch
alters, weeds will grow in old paths and the new waterhole
exist in a new weaving: means, reaching identity too

soon, exclude: mannerism is more suitable to the lyric
than to larger affairs because both lyric and manneristic style
are slight completions: dropping back from the completion

to a linear mode can be more engrossing: for example, the
dactyllic hexameter can grind on, entangling, ingesting bits,
threads, strings, lesser saliences into considerable scope: or

iambic pentameter, especially unrhymed, is an infinitely various

loyable means: one must be ever in search of the rapier that
olds the world on guard: but the sparrow trap traps a sparrow:

disquisition is sesquipedalian pedestrianism, tidying up
he loose bits, but altogether missing the import of the impetus):
center's absolute, if relative: but every point in spacetimematter's

center: reality is abob with centers: indeed, there is
othing but centers: centers of galaxies, systems, planets, asteroids,
moons, drifts, atoms, electrons: and the center, as of the

arth, where all turns and pressures meet, is inexpressibly light,
ill, and empty: the spruce trees at this moment deeply
way with snow and snow is falling, the temperature below

eezing: the muffled morning offered no relief: now, though;
ust after noon, small gusts twist the branches: not
he heavy lower branches, too long in their holding, and too wide,

respond: but twist the lighter, higher branches so they drop
lls of snow and those falls, light, their efficacy increased
y falling, strike the lower, heavier loads, dislodging airy

valanches, sketchy with event but releasing: it seems to me
possibility of unceasing magnitude that these structures
ermit these eventualities: small winds with small branches can

osen heavy postures: a miraculous increase, as if heat could
o uphill: but occurring within a larger frame, at great potential
pense: (but energy displacements, switches, translations are

o considerable for calculation in the smallest sector): still,
ough the whole may be running down, spills
ere and there are overspills, radiances: the lyric, then,

as never been found out because at the center it, too, is
mpty, still, silent: this is a point of provisional
mmation: hence, the *then's, still's,* and *but's:*

point of entangling toward the intertwining of a core, a core
volving every thread: so far, we have ranch, snowsquall,

avalanche, ice skates, wind, etc.: but the main confluence

is one:many which all this essay is about: I get lost for fun,
because there's no chance of getting lost: I am seeking the
mechanisms physical, physiological, epistemological, electrical,

chemical, esthetic, social, religious by which many, kept
discrete as many, expresses itself into the
manageable rafters of salience, lofts to comprehension, breaks

out in hard, highly informed suasions, the "gathering
in the sky" so to speak, the trove of mind, tested
experience, the only place there is to stay, where the saints

are known to share accord and wine, and magical humor floats
upon the ambient sorrow: much is nearly stable there,
residencies perpetual, more than less, where gold is utterly

superfluous and paves the superfluous streets, where phenomena
lose their drift to the honey of eternity: the holy bundle of
the elements of civilization, the Sumerians said: the place

where change is mere disguise, where whatever turns turns
in itself: there is no reason for confusion: that is
what this is about: it's simple and impossibly difficult,

simple by grandeur, impossible by what all must answer there:
enterprise is our American motif, riding horseback between
the obscure beginning and the unformulated conclusion, thinking

grace that show of riding, the expertise, performance, the intricacy
of dealing: to be about something: history can assign and glean,
furnish sources and ends, give grades: that is the

enterprise of history, always best when best accomplished: since
the one thing we learn from history is that we do not learn:
enterprise then's the American salience, rainbow arch,

colossus: but the aristoi are beauty, wealth, birth, genius &
virtue who should be gouvernors: enterprise somewhat, though
not necessarily, inconsistent with those, we lack governors:

he definition of definition goes two ways, opposing:
ne direction cuts away, eliminating from relevance, limits
ito true: take the word *true:* it goes back through ME.

eue, trewe to AS. *treowe, trywe* to a kinship with G. *treu*
nd on to IE. *derew,* meaning tree, in the basic sense of as
rm as a tree: if one could be sure of Indo-European forests

ne might add lofty, abundant, straight, strong, majestic:
omewhere then in the essence of *tree* has been found the
ssence of *true,* including perhaps the perpendicularity or

erticality of true: but while *tree* clarifies the
nind with certain boundaries, it also recalls clusters
f tree-images, memories of particular

rees, and a sense of a translation (separation) in the mind which
s trying to distil *tree,* a luminous, ideal image-tree, the truest
ree, from the actual clusters of memory: it is necessary

hen to turn the essential image of a tree into the truest
ational wordage: truth, then, might be "conformity
vith the facts": but then we know that facts have truth

vhen touched, given configuration by transforming,
nforming fiction: is this unnecessarily
uzzling: all I mean to suggest is that the reality under

vords (and images) is too multiple for rational assessment and
hat language moves by sailing over: the
ther way definition has is to accept the multiplicity of

ynthesis: of course, synthesis is at work in certain levels of
nalysis, but I mean by synthesis the primary intent: look
it it this way: I am experiencing at the moment several

:lusters of entanglement: if I took a single thread from a
ingle cluster, viewed it, explained it, presented it, would
not be violating my reality into artificial clarity and my

undles into artificial linearity: but if I broached, as I seem

to be doing, too many clusters, would I not be violating this
typewriter's mode into nonsense: hue a middle way, the voice

replied, which is what I'm doing the best I can,
that is to say, with too many linking verbs: the grandest
clustering of aggregates permits the finest definition: so out

of that bind, I proceed a little way into similarity and
withdraw a bit into differentiae: unfortunately, man cannot
do better though it might be better done: if I begin with

the picture of a lyre, translate it into a thousand words,
do I have a lyric: what is a lyre-piece: a brief and single
cry: the quickest means to a still point in motion:

three quatrains rhyming alternate lines: let me see if I can
write a poem to help heave the point:

At Once

> Plumage resembles foliage
> for camouflage often
> and so well at times it's difficult
>
> to know whether nature means
> resembler or resembled:
> obviously among things is
>
> included the preservation of
> distinction in a seeming oneness:
> I say it not just
>
> because I often have: maximum
> diversity with maximum unity
> prevents hollow easiness.

                                        poetry, even in its
self-rationale aims two ways at once, polar ways sometimes

to heighten the crisis and pleasure of the reconciliation:

getting back to *tree* and *true*, though, I was thinking last
June, so multiple and dense is the reality of a tree, that I

ought to do a booklength piece on the elm in the backyard here:
I wish I had done it now because it could stand for truth, too:
I did do a sketch one day which might suggest the point:

    I guess it's a bit airy to get mixed up with
    an elm tree on anything
    like a permanent basis: but I've had it
        worse before—talking stones and bushes—and may
        get it worse again: but in this one
    the elm doesn't talk: it's just an object, albeit
      hard to fix:
    unfixed, constantly
    influenced and influencing, still it hardens and enters
    the ground at a fairly reliable point:
especially since it's its
general unalterability that I need to define and stress
       I ought to know its longitude and latitude,
so I could keep checking them out: after all, the ground
drifts:
and rises: and maybe rises slanting—that would be
difficult to keep track of, the angle
      could be progressive or swaying or
seasonal, underground rain
& "floating" a factor: in hilly country
      the underground mantle, the
"float" bedrock is in, may be highly variable and variable
in effect:
I ought to know the altitude, then, from some fixed point:
I assume the fixed point would have to be
    the core center of the planet, though I'm perfectly
prepared to admit the core's involved
    in a slow—perhaps universal—slosh that would alter the
    center's position
    in terms of some other set of references I do not
    think I will at the moment entertain
    since to do so invites an outward, expanding

reticulation
too much to deal precisely with:

true, I really ought to know where the tree is: but I know
it's in my backyard:
I've never found it anywhere else and am willing to accept
            the precision of broadness: with over-precision
things tend to fade: but since I do need stability and want
to make the tree stand for that (among other things)
it seems to me I ought to be willing to learn enough about
theory and instrument
to take sights for a few days or weeks and see if anything
roundly agreeable could be winnowed out: that
ought to include altimeters (several of them, to average
instrumental variation), core theory and gravity waves:
but I'm convinced I'm too awkward
and too set in some ways
to take all that on: if I am to celebrate multiplicity,
unity, and such
I'll be obliged to free myself by accepting certain
limitations:

            I am just going to take it for granted
            that the tree is in the backyard:
it's necessary to be quiet in the hands of the marvelous:

I am impressed with the gradualism of sway,
of growth's sway: the bottom limb that John's
swing's on and that's largely horizontal
has gradually outward toward the tip
    demonstrated the widening of the leaves
by
sinking: the rate of sinking, which is the rate of
growth, has been
within the variations of night and day, rain and shine,
broadly constant
and the branch's adjustment to that growth
    of a similar order: nevertheless, the
wind has lifted, a respiratory floating, the branch
as if all the leaves had breathed in, many a
time
and let it fall

ld rain and dew have often lowered it below its depth—
irds have lighted bringing
arying degrees of alteration to the figurings, sharp
istortions, for example, to the
wigs, slow dips to secondary branches, perhaps no
oticeable effect at the branch root:
          I should go out and measure the diameters of
ie branch, secondary branches, small limbs, and twigs
id their extensions from base
id devise a mathematics
o predict the changes of located average birds: it
ould give me plenty to do for weeks
id save me from the rigors of many heights:
r scoot me to them: conceiving a fact stalls the
nagination to its most threatening dimension:

think now of growth at the edges of the leaves as the
everse of the elmworm's forage:

ie elmworm, I haven't seen any this year—one spring
iere were millions—is as to weight an interesting
eculation:
5 he eats the leaf lessens but of course the weight is
lded to himself, so on a quick scale the
ansformation is one to one:
ut the worm makes waste, the efficiency of his mechanisms
verage and wasteful: in the long range, then,
orms lighten trees and let in light: but that's
iother problem: could it be maintained that
ie worm lets in light enough
o increase growth equal to his destruction:
  it's a good point, a true variable, but surely
iy sudden defoliation by a plague of worms
ould be harmful: a re-entry of winter (though possibly
ith all of winter's possibility): time and number figure
iysteriously here:

ne should be patient and note large results,
eserve some time for broad awareness:

road awareness is the gift of settled minds: or of
iinds hurt high from painful immediacy: it eliminates

and jettisons
sensory contact with too much accident and event—total
    dependencies at the edge: the man
fully aware,
unable to separate out certain large motions, probably
couldn't move: it's better, I think, to be
broadly and emptily aware so as more efficiently
to negotiate the noons of recurrence:

(I have come lately to honor gentleness so:
it's because
of my engagement with
tiny sets and systems of energy, nucleations and constructs,
that I'm unnerved with the slight and needful
    of consideration: part of consideration's
slightness: it approaches and stands off peripherally
quiet and patient should a gesture
be all that's right
            but of course it will on invitation tend:
            it never blunts or overwhelms with aid
            or transforms in order to be received):

while shade increases equally with surface area of leaf
the net result's
a considerable variance:
leaves inter-shade
but the result on the ground's non-accumulative:

in May last year, a month before the above sketch, I did another
briefer thing:

            elm seed, maple
            seed shower
            loose when the wind
            stirs, a spring-wind harvesting
            (when so many things
            have to be picked—take strawberries,
            stooped to and crawled
            along before, or the finger-bluing
            of blueberries):

everything so
gentle and well
done: I sit down not to flaw
the ambience:

the elm seed's winged all round
and exists, a sheathed
swelling, in the center: it
can flutter,
spin,
or, its axis just right, slice
with a draft or cut through one:
(it doesn't go very far but it can
get out of the shade):

then there's the maple seed's oar-wing:
it spins too
(simply, on an ordinary day)
but in a gust can glide broadside:

(dandelion seeds in a head are
noted for their ability to become detached
though attached:
with a tiny splint-break
the wind can have a bluster of them:
the coming fine of an intimation):

those are facts, one-sided extensions:
since the wind's indifferent
the seeds take pains to
make a difference:
praise god for the empty and undesigned:

      hampered by being ungreat poetry, incapable of
arrying quick conviction into imagination's locked clarity,

evertheless these pieces establish the point
at a book might be written on the interpenetrations of
ppearance of an elm tree, especially when the seasons could be

brought in, the fluff cresting snow limbs, the stars and the
influence of starlight on growth or stunting—I have no
idea how such distance affects leaves—the general surround, as of

wind, rain, air pollution, bird shade, squirrel nest: books
by the hundred have already been written on cytology, the
study of cells, and in an elm tree there are twelve quintillion cells,

especially in the summer foliage, and more takes place by way
of event, disposition and such in a single cell than any computer
we now have could keep registration of, given the means of deriving

the information: but if I say books could be written about a single
tree I mean to say only that truth is difficult, even when
noncontradicting; that is, the mere massive pile-up of information

is recalcitrant to higher assimilations without great loss of
concretion, without wide application of averaging: things are
reduced into knowledge: and truth, as some kind of lofty reification,

is so great a reduction it is vanished through by spirit only, a
parallelogram, square or beam of light, or perhaps a more casual
emanation or glow: when so much intellectual energy seems to be

coming to nothing, the mind searches its culture clutch for meaningful
or recurrent objects, finds say a crown or flag or apple or tree or
beaver and invests its charge in that concretion, that focus: then

the symbol carries exactly the syrup of many distillations and
hard endurance, soft inquiry and turning: the symbol apple and the
real apple are different apples, though resembled: "no ideas but in

things" can then be read into alternatives—"no things but in ideas,"
"no ideas but in ideas," and "no things but in things": one thing
always to keep in mind is that there are a number of possibilities:

whatever sways forward implies a backward sway and the mind must
either go all the way around and come back or it must be prepared
to fall back and deal with the lost sway, the pressure for dealing

increasing constantly with forwardness: it's surprising to me

at my image of the orders of greatness comes in terms of descent:
would call the lyric high and hard, a rocky loft, the slow,

owline melt of individual crystalline drops, three or four to
e lyric: requires precision and nerve, is almost always badly
complished, but when not mean, minor: then there is the rush,

ttle, and flash of brooks, pyrotechnics that turn water white:
oetry is magical there, full of verbal surprise and dashed
tonishment: then, farther down, the broad dealing, the smooth

llness of the slow, wide river: there starts the show of genius,
motion, massive beyond the need of disturbing surprise, but, still,
anneled by means—the land's—other than its own: genius, and

e greatest poetry, is the sea, settled, contained before the first
rrent stirs but implying in its every motion adjustments
roughout the measure: one recognizes an ocean even from a dune and

e very first actions of contact with an ocean say ocean over and
er: read a few lines along the periphery of any of the truly
eat and the knowledge delineates an open shore:

hat is to be gained from the immortal person except the experience
ocean: take any line as skiff, break the breakers, and go out
to the landless, orientationless, but perfectly contained, try

e suasions, brief dips and rises, and the general circulations,
e wind, the abundant reductions, stars, and the experience is
tained: but rivers, brooks, and trickles have their uses and

ecial joys and achieve, in their identities, difficult absoluteness:
t will you say, what of the content—why they are all made of water:
t will you, because of the confusion, bring me front center as

mere mist or vapor: charity is greater than poetry: enter it,
consideration of my need and weakness: I find I am able to say
nly what is in my head: a heady constraint: and to say it only

well as I can: inventory my infirmities and substitute
our love for them, and let us hold on to one another and

move right away from petulant despair: to broach a summary, I

would say the problem is scientific—how is reality to be
rendered: how is 4,444 to be made 444 and 44 and 4 and 1: I
have the shaky feeling I've just said something I don't trust:

poems are arresting in two ways: they attract attention with
glistery astonishment and they hold it: stasis: they gather and
stay: the progression is from sound and motion to silence and

rest: for example, I can sit in this room, close my eyes, and
reproduce the whole valley landscape, still: I can see the
southern end of Lake Cayuga, I can see Stewart Park, the highways,

the breaking out and squaring up of Ithaca, I can see the hill-ridges
rising from the Lake, trees, outcroppings of rocks, falls, ducks
and gulls, the little zoo, the bridges: I can feel my eyesight

traveling around a held environment: I am conscious that the
landscape is fixed at the same time that I can move around in it:
a poem is the same way: once it is thoroughly known, it contains

its motion and can be reproduced whole, all its shapeliness intact,
to the mind at the same time the mind can travel around in it and
know its sound and motion: nothing defined can

be still: the verbal moves, depends there, or sinks into unfocused
irreality: ah, but when the mind is brought to silence, the
non-verbal, and the still, it's whole again to see how motion goes:

the left nest in the shrub has built up a foothigh cone of snow
this morning and four sparrows sitting in the quince bush are
the only unaugmented things around: eight more inches are piling

on to ten we had and every evergreen has found the way it would
lean in a burden, split its green periphery and divide: John's
old tractor on the lawn only shows its steering wheel: the

snowplow's been by and blocked the driveway: it's December 26:
yesterday was Christmas: I got a pair of water-resistant gloves
with a removable woolen lining: I got Phyllis three charms for

ιe bracelet I bought her in Rome: John got a snowsled, a beautiful
ooden train set, Lincoln logs, toggles, and several things
ɔerated by non-included batteries: this morning he has no fever:

ε's had tonsillitis this is the fifth day with fevers to 103 and
ɔ4: I've felt built over a jerking machine, not quite turned on
ɪ off: this morning John put on his new cowboy hat (he's nearly

ɔur) and I put on his crash helmet, and we searched all the dark
orners and closets for thieves and robbers: we jailed a couple:
ne teddy bear and one stuffed, long-legged leprechaun: everyone

ʲill find here a detail that is a key to a set of memories:
ɹrings of nucleations please me more than representative details:
ɪot that the detail is representative—only that it is a detail

f numerical dominance in recurrence):

> subatomic particle
> atom
> molecule
> cell
> tissue
> organ
> organ system
> organism
> species
> community
> living world

or

> observation
> problem
> hypothesis
> experiment
> theory
> natural law:

the swarm at the

ɪbatomic level may be so complex and surprising that it puts quasars, pulsars and other matters to shame: I don't know:

and "living world" on the other hand may be so scanty in its
information as to be virtually of no account: nevertheless,
a drift is expressed in the progressions up or down—organization,

the degree of: the control into integration (integrated action)
of the increasingly multiple: the human organism, composed of
billions of cells formed into many specializations and subordinations,

can deliver its total lust to the rarification of sight of the
beloved: for example: and many other high levels of symmetry,
unification, and concerted thrust: poems, of human make, are

body images, organisms of this human organism: if that isn't
so I will be terribly disappointed: it sounds as if it ought to
be right: consonants, vowels, idioms, phrases, clauses (tissues),

sentences (organs), verses (organ systems), poems (living worlds):
I react to such stuff with a burst of assent resembling for all
I can tell valuable feeling: rubbing a girl also, of course,

produces feeling, I would be the last to deny it, but it may be
precisely the organization-principle in girls that one, rubbing,
is pleasured by: if, as I believe, we are not only ourselves—i.e.,

the history of our organism—but also every process that went into
our making, then, in the light of our present ignorance, we may
safely leave much potentiality to undisclosed possibility: mush,

mush, how friendly: that's what I think, I'll tell you in a nut-
shell: and in poems, the insubstantial processes of becoming
form inscrutable parts of the living thing: and then how the

orders of the poem build up and cooperate into the pure heat of
sight and insight, trembling and terror: it makes me gasp aghast:
no wonder we pedants talk about history, influence, meaning

in poems: that's peripheral enough to prevent the commission of
larger error, and safe error is a pedantic preference well-known,
widely footnoted, and amply rewarded: I believe in fun:

"superior amusement" is a little shitty: fun is nice: it's what
our society is built on: fun in the enterprise: I believe in it:
I have no faith in the scoffers: they are party-poopers who are

afraid they ought to believe in history or logical positivism and
don't have any real desire to do so: they are scarcely worth a
haircut: organisms, I can tell you, build up under the thrust to

joy and nothing else can lift them out of the miry circumstance:
and poems are pure joy, however divisionally they sway with grief:
the way to joy is integration's delivery of the complete lode:

the flow broken, coinless, I, the third morning of Ithaca's most
historical snowbind, try to go on, difficult, difficult, the hedges
split open, showing inside the vacancy and naked, bony limbs: snow

up past the garage door handle, new snow still falling, and high
gusts roaring through the cold: supplies low or gone: and the stores
closed: that last appeals too much in the wrong sort: like any

scholar, I should, at this point to uncripple the condition, quote,
but first, I must, like a scholar, clear the field: I choose Ruskin
to say what thousands have said: "Art is neither to be achieved by

effort of thinking, nor explained by accuracy of speaking": well,
still, Ruskin, it cannot be achieved without effort, and one level
of accuracy may be preferred to another: this must be a point of

clustering because I feel a lot of little things jostling
to get in where they can be said: for example, I just walked
a mile to the store, blowing snow, I was in to my ass practically

getting out to the plowed road: I got hotdogs, bacon, bread (out of
eggs), coffee: and on the way back, the wind in my face and snow
drifted ten feet high along one curve that has an open field behind

it, I passed two straggly young girls laughing, dogs barking after
them, and one carrying her jacket, big boobs jouncing in her short-
sleeved sweater: I was barking inside myself a little, rosy ideas

in the blinding snowlight: one guy I passed said "beautiful weather"—

the kind of thing one, after four days penned up, is grateful to
say and hear: I quote now to enrich the mix, to improve my stew from

the refrigerator of timeless ingredients:

> "A large number of the inhabitants of a mud flat will be
> worms. It is hard to develop enthusiasm for worms, but it took
> nature more than a billion years to develop a good worm—
> meaning one that has specialized organs for digestion, respi-
> ration, circulation of the blood and excretion of wastes.
> All organisms perform these functions—amoebas, flagellates,
> bacteria or even filterable viruses; but the worms—at least
> the higher worms—do all these things better. They also de-
> veloped segmentation or reduplication of parts, permitting in-
> crease in size with completely coordinated function. Contem-
> porary architects call this modular construction. It is found in
> man in the spinal column, in the segmental arrangement of
> spinal nerves, and in some other features that are especially
> prominent during embryonic development."

> *The Sea* by Robert C. Miller. Random House. New York,
> 1966. p. 165.

> "We may sum up. Carbohydrates, fats, proteins, nucleic
> acids, and their various derivatives, together with water and
> other inorganic materials, plus numerous additional com-
> pounds found specifically in particular types of living matter
> —these are the molecular bricks out of which living matter is
> made. To be sure, a mere random pile of such bricks does not
> make a living structure, any more than a mere pile of real
> bricks makes a house. First and foremost, if the whole is to be
> living, the molecular components must be organized into a
> specific variety of larger microscopic bodies; and these in turn,
> into actual, appropriately structured cells."

> *The Science of Botany* by Paul B. Weisz and Melvin S.
> Fuller. McGraw-Hill Book Company, Inc., 1962. p. 48.

                              poems are verbal
symbols for these organizations: they imprint upon the mind
examples of integration in which the energy flows with maximum

effect and economy between the high levels of oneness and the
numerous subordinations and divisions of diversity: it is simply
good to have the mind exposed to and reflected by such examples:

it firms the mind, organizes its energy, and lets the controlled
flows occur: that is simple good in itself: I can't stress that
enough: it is not good for something else—although of course

it is good for infinite things else: so my point is that the poem
is the symbolical representation of the ideal organization, whether
the cell, the body politic, the business, the religious

group, the university, computer, or whatever: I used to wonder
why, when they are so little met and understood, poems are taught
in schools: they are taught because they are convenient examples

of the supreme functioning of one and many in an organization of
cooperation and subordination: young minds, if they are to "take
their place in society" need to learn patience—that oneness is

not useful when easily derived, that manyness is not truthful when
thinly selective—assent, that the part can, while insisting on
its own identity, contribute to the whole, that the whole can

sustain and give meaning to the part: and when these things
are beautifully—that is, well—done, pleasure is a bonus
truth-functioning allows: that is why art is valuable: it is

extremely valuable: also, in its changing, it pictures how
organizations can change, incorporate innovation, deal with accidence
and surprise, and maintain their purpose—increasing the means and

assuring the probability of survival: the point of change, though,
brings me to a consideration of the adequacy of the transcendental
vegetative analogy: the analogy is so appealing, so swept with

conviction, that I hardly ever have the strength to question it:
I've often said that a poem in becoming generates the laws of its
own becoming: that certainly sounds like a tree, growing up with

no purpose but to become itself (regardless of the fact that many

are constantly trying to turn it into lumber): but actually, a tree
is a print-out: the tree becomes exactly what the locked genetic

code has pre-ordained—allowing, of course, for variables of weather,
soil, etc.: so that the idea that some organic becoming is
realizing itself in the vegetative kingdom is only partially

adequate: real change occurs along the chromosomes, a risky business
apparently based on accidence, chance, unforeseeable distortion:
the proportion of harmful to potentially favorable mutations is

something like 50,000 to 1: how marvelous that the possibility of
favorable change is a flimsy margin in overwhelming, statistically,
destruction and ruin: that is the way nature pours it on: once it

has arrived at a favorable organization—a white oak, for example—
it does not allow haphazard change to riddle it—no, it protects the
species by the death of thousands of its individuals: but lets the

species buy by the hazard of its individuals the capacity to adjust,
should adjustment be indicated or allowed: that is terrifying and
pleasing: a genetic cull myself, I have the right to both

emotions: along the periphery of integrations, then, is an exposure
to demons, thralls, witcheries, the maelstrom black of
possibility, costly, chancy, lethal, open: so I am not so much

arguing with the organic school as shifting true organismus from
the already organized to the bleak periphery of possibility,
an area transcendental only by its bottomless entropy: a word on the

art/nature thing: art is the conscious preparation for the unconscious
event: to the extent that it is possible—a fining up of the attention
and filling out of the means: art is the craft and lore of preparing

the soil for seed: no enmity: complementary: is any yeoman
dumb enough to think that by much cultivation of the fields wheat
will sprout: or that saying words over the barren, the seedless,

will make potatoes: son of a gun's been keeping a bag of seed-wheat
in the barn all winter, has sorted out good potatoes and knows how
to cut their eyes out: it's hard to say whether the distinguishers

or the resemblancers are sillier: they work with noumena every
day, but speak of the invisible to them and they laugh with
silver modernity: well, as I said, we are more certain that we

are about than what we are about: here is something I have always
wanted to quote:

> "Around the mouths of rivers, where the fresh waters of the
> land meet the salt waters of the sea, live some of the world's
> densest populations. This food-rich borderland harbors
> immense numbers and varieties of living creatures—proto-
> zoans, worms, snails, shrimp, clams, oysters and on up
> through the vertebrate fishes. Life in an estuary may be rich,
> but it is also almost inconceivably dangerous. The temperature
> of its shallow waters runs the scale from freezing to over 100
> degrees Fahrenheit. Twice each day the ebb and flow of the
> tides drastically alter the conditions of life, sometimes strand-
> ing whole populations to die a high-and-dry or freezing death.
> Winds, floods, and tidal currents often bury the stationary
> bottom animals under suffocating slides of sand or silt. But the
> greatest hazard of all is alien water—water that is too fresh
> or too salty. Aquatic animals are sensitive to the salt content
> of their water environment. A sudden rain-fed flood of fresh
> water from a river mouth can be catastrophic to populations
> dwelling in the estuary."

> "The Life of an Estuary" by Robert M. Ingle. *Scientific
> American*, May 1954.

isn't that beautiful: it has bearing in many
ways on my argument: it provided me years ago with ideas on

risks and possibilities: well, my essay is finished: I thank it
with all my heart for helping me to get through this snowstorm:
having a project is useful especially during natural suspensions.

Two Possibilities

Coming out of the earth and going
into the earth compose

an interval or arc where
what to do's

difficult to fix: if it's
the coming
out that answers, should one with all
thrust come out and

rise to imagination's limit, leaving
earthiness, maximally
to mark the change, much below:
if it's

going in, should one flatten out on
coming, lie low
among bush
and rock, and keep the residence

near the palm of the hand, the
gross engrossed and palpable:
well, there is an interval designed,
apparently, for design.

Plunder

I have appropriated the windy twittering of aspen leaves
into language, stealing something from reality like a
silverness: drop-scapes of ice from peak sheers:

much of the rise in brooks over slow-rolled glacial stones:
the loop of reeds over the shallow's edge when birds
feed on the rafts of algae: I have taken right out of the

air the clear streaks of bird music and held them in my
head like shifts of sculpture glint: I have sent language
through the mud roils of a raccoon's paws like a net,

netting the roils: made my own uses of a downwind's
urgency on a downward stream: held with a large scape
of numbness the black distance upstream to the mountains

flashing and bursting: meanwhile, everything else, frog,
fish, bear, gnat has turned in its provinces and made off
with its uses: my mind's indicted by all I've taken.

Triphammer Bridge

I wonder what to mean by *sanctuary*, if a real or
apprehended place, as of a bell rung in a gold
surround, or as of silver roads along the beaches

of clouds seas don't break or black mountains
overspill; jail: ice here's shapelier than anything,
on the eaves massive, jawed along gorge ledges, solid

in the plastic blue boat fall left water in: if I
think the bitterest thing I can think of that seems like
reality, slickened back, hard, shocked by rip-high wind:

sanctuary, sanctuary, I say it over and over and the
word's sound is the one place to dwell: that's it, just
the sound, and the imagination of the sound—a place.

Lollapalooza: 22 February

Lord, have mercy! what a day: what a merciful day:
went to fifty: I listened all day to garage-music:
old roof snow, heavy-bottomed with melt and freeze,

began at sunrise to drop at the eaves, each drop
discrete as a plectrum: then the old icicles
loosened at the root and fell into brown chrysanthemum

stalks (and snapdragons, still green!) and then as
morning tided, seeing down the angle of the drops
was like watching a rain section, and then by noon,

the wind risen, the eaves swung ragged with sound
and glitter: I felt the roof rise as if to relief,
ten weeks turning casually to water: the afternoon

was lovely and constant (except, wingfeathers in a
ground-melt, I shoved the mound aside to find, as if alive,
a pheasant under snow): at dusk, a patch of white

still centered on the roof, I went out to check and
sure enough the motions had lessened: spicule icicles
lengthened into a lessening overflow, the music cold-skimpy.

The City Limits

When you consider the radiance, that it does not withhold
itself but pours its abundance without selection into every
nook and cranny not overhung or hidden; when you consider

that birds' bones make no awful noise against the light but
lie low in the light as in a high testimony; when you consider
the radiance, that it will look into the guiltiest

swervings of the weaving heart and bear itself upon them,
not flinching into disguise or darkening; when you consider
the abundance of such resource as illuminates the glow-blue

bodies and gold-skeined wings of flies swarming the dumped
guts of a natural slaughter or the coil of shit and in no
way winces from its storms of generosity; when you consider

that air or vacuum, snow or shale, squid or wolf, rose or lichen,
each is accepted into as much light as it will take, then
the heart moves roomier, the man stands and looks about, the

leaf does not increase itself above the grass, and the dark
work of the deepest cells is of a tune with May bushes
and fear lit by the breadth of such calmly turns to praise.

Satyr Formalist

As the perpetual laughter about the grounds,
the grouped yews and carved high stones (always
in a diminishment, looking for light),

as the caperer of flat stones, their intervals
a watery disarray nevertheless along directions, the
light dunker of lilypad leaves (to see the jewels

roll in and stand), as the caresser of whatever
gets too far into the dark, the whickerer at
hints of gross intent, sampler of hues and

cornices, he touched death for the first time as
the smallest significance of a tremble in the thighs,
the rounding white of the moon in his eyes, stricture

by the thornbush border, and uncomprehending, like
us, uncomprehending, he took to it blank, vacancy
to vacancy, brittle, fine, dew-bush's pool drop.

Late Romantic

Change the glacier's loneliness and the ice melts,
streams going off into sundry identity systems,
bog floats, lakes, clouds, seas, drinking water:

flux heightens us into knots of staid tension:
we live and go about containing various swirls:
too much swirling improves loneliness poorly:

we take advantage of separateness to unite sensible
differences, the tube in the fineness of its coupling
nearly a merging: well, nothing's perfect: fall

away, of course—we have other things to do alone,
go to the bathroom, brush our teeth, reel:
how can we give ourselves away if we're not separate

enough to be received: and, given away, we know
no desire but the other's desire: and given each
to each, we're both both, indistinguishably, sort of.

Spaceship

It's amazing all
this motion going
on and
water can lie still
in glasses and the gas
can in the
garage doesn't rattle.

Cleavage

Soon as
you stop
having trouble
getting down
to earth
you start
having trouble
getting off
the ground

Schooling

Out mountainward, I explained I've already
yielded to so much, truly, an abundance,

to seas, of course, ranges, glaciers, large
rivers, to the breadth of plains, easily to

outcroppings of bedrock, specially those
lofted amalgamated magmas, grainy, dense, and

easily to waterfalls double-hands can't halt:
but now I'm looking to yield to lesser

effects, wind-touch of a birch branch, for
example, weed-dip, tilting grasses in seed,

the brush of a slipped lap of lakewater
over a shore stone: I think I'm almost

down to shadows, yielding to their masses,
for my self out here, taut against the mere

suasion of a star, is explaining, dissolving
itself, saying, be with me wind bent at leaf

edges, warp me puddle riffle, show me
the total yielding past shadow and return.

Space Travel

Go down the left
hand side of the yard,
a contrived bankslope,
down to the corner of
the lot, past the
forsythia bushes now
all green, and look
back up toward the house,
the lawn, the young
maple, the bushes along
the foundation & you can
practically work up
a prospect: vision adjusts:
feeling roomy is room
enough and many a
twenty-mile out-west view
thins to staging:
it's going to be all right
I think, for those
who wish to live, at least:
there are some who do.

High Surreal

Spit the pit in the pit
I told the cherry eater
and see what crumbling
shoulders, gully washes,
& several other bardic
dimensions can produce:
possibly a shiny asbestos
tree with cherry
nuts—reversal obvious
in the formation—but
if you come to impossible
productions on
absent trees, get out the
bulldozer and shove the
whole thing over smooth.

Sharp Lookout

Rain still falls, the wind moves
the maple branches to
gestures and patterns reasonable:
the stream deals with rocks
and hollows, slowing or dashing,
in ways apparently regular: whole
bushes and even tall trees
light up as usual with song to
the songbird out of sight:
the clouds that have never taken
shape are shapely: the bulby,
engrossing sun splinters red
through the hedge toward dusk:
though I've been expecting
a wrench or unpraiseworthy re-ordering
to shock loose any moment from
lost curvatures, I've not been able
today to form evidence of any
trend countering our prospects
for a moderate life and a safe death.

Right On

The tamarack can cut rain down to size, mist-little
bead-gauze, hold at needlepoint a plenty
and from the going, blue-sunk storm keep a

shadow, glittery recollection: the heart-leaved
big hydrangea bends over blossom-nodding, a few
large drops and a general glaze streaking leaves

with surface tension: the maple leaves
gather hail-size drops at the lobes and
sway them ragged loose: spirea, quince, cedar,

elm, hollyhock, clover (a sharp beader)
permit various styles of memory: then the sun
breaks out and clears the record of what is gone.

Rectitude

Last night's thunderstorm's
glancing quick shifts of strong wind and
heavy sheets of tensed up
beating down rain

have left the snapdragons
velvet-hung in red bead
bedraggled, a
disorientation extreme:

but this morning,
the clouds clearing, the sun
breaking its one source out,
light is working in the stems' cells,

drawing up, adjusting, soft alignments
coming true, and pretty soon
now the prevailing command "attention!"
will seem to have been uttered suddenly.

Object

X out the rondure of
the totally satisfying
and all other sizable areas
near the central scope:
that degree, that circumference,
put aside: the leftovers,
though, pips & squeaks,
think to pick up, shovel
up, if possible: that is what
is left: stuffing the central
experience into the peripheral
bit overinvests though &
creates aura,
wistfulness and small floating.

Ground Tide

Headed back home from Harold's, we came down
from some Connecticut hills, crossed the
height-slowed Hudson, mounted into the hills

again, the Catskills, made the divide and then
picked up a stream that ironed out
in wandering descent as much as possible into

one grade—when we noticed the earth risen,
darkness of lofted hills, every one piled with
woods and possessed to the top, drowning

us under the dark line of a weighty dominance:
nothing of the sort, of course! just fall-outs
of the ridge we'd already cleared, and so,

amiably, tilted by grade into a floating,
unearned speed, we eased on out into the open
failing slopes, led by the spiritual, risen stream.

Translating

This afternoon the thunderstorms were separate and tall,
the intervals blue with clearing and white with icy
summits moiling upward till height could accept no

more and the vast glides called out evenness: so,
through the afternoon there were several systems of
shower, the translations of heat vapor lofted to grit-ice,

the falling drafts of grit bounding, gathering into stones, the
further falls through the heavy warmer waters: at first, the drops
in any shower were huge, few, obviously stone water,

then the narrower rods of slant-thick rain, then even
smaller rain, dense but fine with a half-light following or
a full breaking out of sun: then, it was, the sun come but

the rain not over, I saw under the aural boughs of the elm
the last translation, a fine-weaving gathered by leaves,
augmented from tip to tip into big, lit, clear, sparse drops.

Sorting

There's not much hill left up from here and after
rains runlets lose head quickly to the least
quiver: height has such poverty of

reservoir, and in a drought poplars will go
brittle with yearning and take lightly their usual
mass and rock-hold, while at the bottom of the

ridge, the fountains will still be blinking,
the glade weeds rushed green: well, at least, we get
some view up here and sometimes breezes that miss

the valley cut a high sweep across from ridge to ridge
and then most often the drought will break
in time, the trees come back, a branch or two burnished.

The Next Day

Morning glory vine
slight
as it is will
double on itself and
pile over
a quince bush before
you know it:
so the woodless-stemmed
can
by slender travel
arrange its leaves and
take away
light from the wooded:
beholding the rampancy
and the
thin-leaved quince
thereunder, I stripped
off an armload
of vine
and took it down to
the brushheap
under the pear tree:
the next day
the wilted leaves had
given up their
moisture to the
vines that here and
there
to diminished glory
lifted half-opened
morning glory blooms.

Extremes and Moderations

Hurly-burly: taking on whatever is about to get off, up the
slack, ready with prompt-copy for the reiteration, electronic
to inspect the fuzzy-buffoon comeback, picking up the diverse
gravel of mellifluous banality, the world-replacing world

world-irradiating, lesser than but more outspoken:
constructing the stanza is not in my case exceedingly
difficult, variably invariable, permitting maximum change
within maximum stability, the flow-breaking four-liner, lattice

of the satisfactory fall, grid seepage, currents distracted
to side flow, multiple laterals that at some extreme spill
a shelf, ease back, hit the jolt of the central impulse: the
slow working-down of careful investigation, the run

diffused, swamped into variable action: my ideal's a cold
clod clam calm, clam contained, nevertheless active in the
digestion, capable of dietary mirth, the sudden whisk, nearly
rollably spherical: ah, but friends, to be turned

loose on an accurate impulse! how handsome the stanzas are
beginning to look, open to the total acceptance, fracturing into
delight, tugging down the broad sweep, thrashing it into
particulars (within boundaries): diversity, however—as of

the concrete—is not ever-pleasing: I've seen fair mounds
of fine-stone at one end or the other of highway construction
many times and been chiefly interested in the "hill": but
abstraction is the bogey-boo of those incapable of it, while,

merrily, every abstractor brings the concrete up fine: one,
anyway, as Emerson says, does well what one settles down to:
it's impossible anyone should know anything about the concrete
who's never risen above it, above the myth of concretion

in the first place: pulverize such, unequal to the synthesis,
the organism by which they move and breathe their particulars:
and the symbol won't do, either: it differentiates flat
into muffling fact it tried to stabilize beyond: there aren't

just problems for the mind, the mind's problematic, residing
here by a scary shading merely: so much so it does seem
at times to prefer an origin other-worldly, the dreaminess,
the surficial hanging-on, those interior swirls nearly

capable of another invention: astonishingly, the
celestial bodies are round, not square or triangular, not

dodecahedral, and then they are sprinkled in the void's
unusual abundance: if it weren't for light, we wouldn't think

anything here, that scanty a fabric: that is the way it
was made: worse, that is the way it works out: when the lady
said she accepted the universe, it was a sort of decision:
anyway, granted that the matter appears to be settled, there's

plenty around for the mind to dwell on: that's a comfort,
but, now, a ghastly comfort: that's the difference:
the first subject I wanted to introduce, because it's
inanimate but highly active, is my marble garden bench down

by the elm—actually, well under the elm: it's in three parts:
the seat slab, four to five inches thick, and the two end slabs,
equally thick but, deeply buried, of undetermined length: I
bought this old place a few years ago, so wasn't present for the

setting: but as to length the upper slab is, say, four feet:
some cool seeps up the legs from the ground, but I
doubt there's much commission between the legs and the upper
slab: cool nights deeply penetrate the bench, so that on

a flash-hot summer morning, the reservoir of dense cooling
will ooze right through to one's bottom, providing, I must say,
a tendency to equilibrium: the stone never gets as hot as the
day and never as cool as the night (maybe it's colder some winter

nights of cold remembrances) so it moderates the environment,
working as a heater or air-conditioner: it has no moving
parts—it's all moving parts, none visible—and yet is
capable of effect, animation: that such a thing can work for

us day and night makes us feel, by cracky, that nature is our
servant, though without singular intention: the gift, though,
the abundance! we don't have to pay for, that requires no
matching social security funds, no fringe benefits: the

unutterable avenue of bliss: in spite of the great many works
in progress, I feel this is the last poem to the world: every
poet probably feels he is writing the last poem to the world:
man, in motion how avaricious, has by the exaggeration of his

refinement shown what intelligence can commit in the universe:
bleak scald of lakes, underground poisonous tides, air litter
like a dusk, clouds not like the clouds: can we give our wild
life a brake: must we keep tinkering until a virus swerves

from our interventions into a genesis consummating us: must
we spew out acids till we're their stew: lead on the highways,
washing into the grass, collecting into lead brooklets bound
for diffusive destinations: get your musclebound mercury dose

here: come on, guys: we know how to handle the overpopulation
problem: sell folks carloads of improvement marked uncertain:
progress can be the end of us: how neat: in a way, you might
say, how right, how just, poetically just: but come on, I say,

overrefined exaggeration, if you got us into this, can't you
get us out: come on, hot-shot fusion: give us plenty with no
bitter aftertaste: paradise lies ahead, where it's always lain:
but we may reach it, before hell overtakes us: nature, if I may

judge out a law, likes extremes, in some ways depends on them, but
usually keeps them short or confined: if we are broadly, densely
extreme, can't we count on the outbreak of dialectical alternatives:
we can count on it: what is a beer party now but a can of cans:

what is wine now but a bottle in a recalcitrant green glow,
empurpling in the sun: nevertheless, the petunias are incarnadine
by the hedgebrush: nevertheless, the catbird comes to the plastic
boat the goldfish summers in, fools around looking, then takes

a drink: we are aided by much I will discuss and much as
yet unfixed: it's time I introduced an extreme, but this time
I'm going to pick a moderate one, I think—the gusts before
thunderstorms: now the gusts before thunderstorms are sometimes

high enough to trim trees: a bough summer has coaxed overweight,
that splitting riddance, serviceable enough, but more anthropo-
centrically, the shaking out of dead branches: when we are
out walking in the woods on a calm day, we don't want a

dead limb to just plunge out of a tree by surprise, striking us,
possibly, on the cranium: whatever we normally go to the woods

for, surely we don't go for that: by high gusts thunderstorms
accomplish the possibility of calm residence: the tree, too,

counts on nodding times, sun-gleanings, free of astonishment,
and to buy them is willing to give up its dead or
even its living limbs: nature gives much on occasion
but exacts a toll, a sacrifice: that puzzling suggestion,

or autumnal impulse, has accounted for much sacred carnage: I
hate to think of it: I nearly hate to think of it: the Maya
hearts pulled out still flicking have always seemed to me gruesome
separations, attention-getting, but god-like with revulsion's awe:

of course, even closer home, high gusts can carry hints to the
hapless by, for example, blowing down a fence obviously too weak
to stand: that should be good news to the farmer whose cows have
been getting out: and who should not be alarmed by an immediate

problem if the lesson has been well bestowed: nature sometimes
gets all its shit together and lets you have it: but good farmers
make good fences and anybody else gets whatever the traffic will
bear away: I wrote the other day a poem on this subject:

> *Ancestors*
> An elm tree, like a society or
> culture, seems to behave out of
> many actions toward a total
> interest (namely, its own) which means
> that in the clutter and calamity
> of days much, locally catastrophic,
> can occur that brings no sharp
> imbalance to the total register:
> for example, dead limbs, white already
> with mold and brackets, can in
> a high storm—the heralding windtwists
> of thunderstorms, say—snap and, though
> decay-light, plunge among the
> lower greens, the many little stiff
> fingers entangling, weighing down
> the structures of growth: ah, what

an insupportable extravagance by
the dead, held off the ground, leaching
white with slow, dry rot: what
a duty for the young limbs, already
crowding and heavy with green: well,
I guess the elm is by that much local
waste wasted, but then perhaps its
sacrifice is to sway in some deep rich
boughs the indifferent, superfluous,
recalcitrant, white, prophesying dead.

circulations are moderations, currents triggered by extremes:
we must at all costs keep the circulations free and clear,
open and unimpeded: otherwise, extremes will become trapped,
local, locked in themselves, incapable of transaction: some

extremes, though, *are* circulations, a pity, in that kinds of
staying must then be the counters: for example, when in spring
a gray sandstorm arises over Indiana, circulation becomes
too free and open: hedgerows, even, are important at such times:

they stall the storm just enough for heavy sand to fall out:
but what of the lengthy problem of small sand and, even worse,
of high-rising fine dust: if the storm hits
Pennsylvania, the woods will drag at its foot, then

tilt and capitulate it: heavy suspensions will lose their
directions to gravity quickly but even the fine dust slowing will
sift through the equally numerical leaves, be caught by them,
and the air will be breatheable again by Jersey, west Jersey:

water's carriages act the same way: high narrow valleys, roomless,
propel water along, loosening sometimes substantial boulders: the
mature valleys, wide-bottomed, slow the flow, and
particulate weight falls out: in the ancient flat valleys,

where meanders have cut off into oxbow lakes or little crescents
of difference, the water goes broad and slow and only the
fine stuff in a colloidal float, a high drift, stays out
the ride, hanging finally in long curtains in the gulfs and lagoons:

well, I just, for poetic purposes, wanted to point out the parallel:
parallel too in that even Pennsylvania can't get some of the
high dust, the microscopic grit—settles out with the
floating spiders on Atlantic isles and (too bad for the spiders)

waves: such circulations are average and quite precious: the
sun's the motor, the mechanisms greased by millions of years
of propriety and correction: the place produced deliciously
habitable, a place we found we could grow into: how marvelous!

lightning is one of the finest, sharpest tensions, energy
concentrations: it has to be lean because it leaps far:
how was the separation to be bridged, the charge neutralized,
except by a high-energy construct: gathers the diffuse

energy from clouds and ground and drains it through a
dense crackling: I don't know how it works: it works:
the charges rush together and annihilate each other:
or the charge goes one way, to the ground, or to the

clouds: I'll bet it's one way and to the ground: the
lofted's precarious: the ground is nice and sweet and not
at all spectacular: I wonder if I'm really talking about
the economy of the self, where an extreme can gather up a lot

of stale stuff and mobilize it, immoderate grief,
or racing terror, or a big unification like love chugging
up to the fold: we never talk about anything but ourselves,
objectivity the objective way of talking about ourselves:

O calligraphers, blue swallows, filigree the world
with figure, bring the reductions, the snakes unwinding,
the loops, tendrils, attachments, turn in necessity's precision,
give us the highwire of the essential, the slippery concisions

of tense attentions! go to look for the ocean currents and
though they are always flowing there they are, right in place, if
with seasonal leans and sways: the human body
staying in change, time rushing through, ingestion,

elimination: if change stopped, the mechanisms of
holding would lose their tune: current informs us,

is the means of our temporary stay: ice water at the northern
circle sinks and in a high wall like a glacier seeps down the

ocean bottom south: but the south's surface water is going
north, often in spiral carriages of an extreme intensity, nevertheless
moderating, preventing worse extremes: as when snow streaks up the
summit, up past the timberline where interference is slight, and

having passed the concision of the ridge, blooms out diffusing
over the valley, drifts out into the catchments, fills with
feathery loads the high ravines, the glacier's compressions forming
underneath, taking direction in the slowest flow of relief, so on

any number of other occasions, massive collections and dispositions
restore ends to sources: O city, I cry at
the gate, the glacier is your
mother, the currents of the deep father you, you sleep

in the ministry of trees, the boulders are your brothers sustaining
you: come out, I cry, into the lofty assimilations: women, let
down your hair under the dark leaves of the night grove, enter
the currents with a sage whining, rising into the circular

dance: men, come out and be with the wind, speedy and lean, fall
into the moon-cheered waters, plunge into the ecstasy of rapids:
children, come out and play in the toys of divinity: glass, brick,
stone, curb, rail are freezing you out of your motions, the

uncluttered circulations: I cry that, but perhaps I am too secular
or pagan: everything, they say, is artificial: nature's the
artwork of the Lord: but your work, city, is aimed unnaturally
against time: your artifice confronts the Artifice: beyond

the scheduled consummation, nothing's to be recalled: there is
memory enough in the rock, unscriptured history in
the wind, sufficient identity in the curve
of the valley: what is your name, city, under your name: who

are your people under their faces: children of the light,
children of the light: of seasons, moons, apples, berries,
grain: children of flies, worms, stars: come out, I cry, into
your parentage, your established natures: I went out and pulled a

few weeds in the lawn: you probably think I was getting goofy
or scared: it was just another show: as the mystic said, it's
all one to me: then I went on over to the University, and there
was Slatoff's new book, fresh from the publisher's: and Kaske

had left me a book he'd told me about: *Ballad of the Bones
and Other Poems*, by Byron Herbert Reece: E.P. Dutton: 1945:
$2.00: introduced by Jesse Stuart: and praised, on
the back cover, by William Rose Benet, John Hall Wheelock,

John Gould Fletcher, and Alfred Kreymborg: I do believe I'm going
to enjoy the book: the South has Mr. Reece and, probably,
Literature: I bet I pulled a thousand weeds: harkweed's
incredible: it puts up a flower (beautiful) to seed but at the

same time sends out runners under the grass that anchor a few
inches or a foot away, and then the leaves of the new plants
press away the grass in a tight fit: I put havoc into those
progressions, believe me: plants take their cue and shape

from crowding: they will crowd anything, including close
relatives, brethren and sistren: everybody, if I may switch
tracks, is out to get his: that is the energy we must allow
the widest margin to: and let the margins, then, collide into

sensible adjustments: slow moderations are usually massive:
nature can't heave a lot fast, air and
oceans reasonably unwieldy: true, they work into lesser
intensities, local: maelstroms, typhoons, fairly rapid highs

or lows, the boiling up of deep, cold water: dimension may be
the sorter, although it didn't seem so originally with the
garden bench, small and yet efficiently moderating: if
you built a wall across the Gulf Stream, though, the sundering

would be lengthy: and what would it take to bring about a quick
thermal change in an ocean: a solar burst; at least,
unusual effusion: quantity of mass or number (as of leaves) then
moderates the local effect: as for cooling an ocean, a lot of

icebergs would have to split off from the caps and plunge before
the change would be measurable: expanded, though, through

sufficient time—a massiveness—the lesser effects could assume
large implications: but, of course, with the icebergs, one

would have to investigate the mechanisms that were heating up the
general air, causing the splits in the first place, and then one
would have to deal with the probability that the air, massive to
massive, would warm up the oceans which would then be able to

absorb large numbers of icebergs without cooling: I suppose
my confusion is no more than natural, reflecting
the reticulation of interpenetration in nature, whereby we should
be advised to tamper cautiously with least balances,

lest a considerable number, a series or so, tilt
akimbo: even now, though, we apparently cannot let well enough
alone: how well it was! how computer-like in billionths the
administration and take of the cure: just think, the best cure

would arise by subtle influence of itself if only we would
disappear: but though we have scalded and oiled the seas and
scabbed the land and smoked the mirror of heaven, we must try
to stay and keep those who are alive alive: then we

might propose to ourselves that collectively we have one grain
of sense and see what the proposition summons forth: the force of
the drive by which we have survived is hard to counter, even
now that we survive so densely: and it is not certain the plants

would not lose their shape and vigor if they had to stop
crowding: a very hard reversal and loss of impetus: we may
have time to diminish and cope with our thrust: the little patch
of wildwoods out behind my backhedge is even now squeaky and

chirpy with birds and the day is as clear as a missing windowpane:
the clouds are few, large, and vastly white: the air has no
smell and the shade of trees is sharp: floods are extreme
by narrowing rain, which can, itself, be quite bountiful:

it's hard to blame floods—useless—because they're just
showing how hard they can work to drain the land:
one way a slow impulse works up into an extremity's
the earthquake: coastal land, say, drifts with sea currents

north a couple of inches a year, setting up a strain along a
line with the land's land: at some point, tension gives in
a wrack and wrecks stability, restoring lassitude: or resonance
of circulation coming into a twist or "beat": the gathering up,

the event, the dissipation: but that would imply that everything,
massive, slow, or long is moving toward the enunciation of
an extreme: we dwell in peace on the post-tables and
shelves of these remarkable statements: what kind of lurch is

it, I wonder, when a comet sideswipes us, or swishes by near
enough to switch our magnetic poles: can the atmosphere
be shifted a few hundred miles: the oceans
would pile up and spill: maybe just the magnetic poles would

switch, that sounds all right: but if the comet hit us and
glanced off or even stuck, its impact would affect
our angular momentum and possibly put some wobble in our motion:
somebody said the purpose of science is to put us in control

of our environment, allaying calamity and catastrophe, though
conceivably also making nice days a little nicer: well, all
I say (figuratively speaking) is a lot of things are
still in their own control: maybe my point, though, is that

by and large I prefer the other controls to our own, not
forsaking the possibility that still larger controls
by us might bring about a fair, if slightly artificialized,
paradise someday: from here, it looks like ruin and

destruction either way, more or less: one thing we will never
do is sit around on this planet doing nothing, just soaking
up the honey of solar radiation: if our problems were
solved, we'd go out of business: (stretch that a little

and it will do): it's dry: the weeds in the lawn
are being tested to the limit, some having died: I've just
put a soakhose by the maple: I'll let it go slowly that way
for a few hours: the grass in patches is parched tan:

it crackles underfoot: tight spurs of hay:
I didn't see the hornet at first when I went to attach the

hose: he was sucking the spigot: people around here don't
have sprinklers, I can't understand it: I always used to have

one in South Jersey: maybe water's expensive or maybe
very dry spells are rare: seems to me I remember a very dry
one last year: the days are shortening: it's sundown
now at eight: maybe a little later officially, but the sun's

down behind the ridge on the other side of the lake by then: any
night could turn sharp cold—read August 21: I've been at this
poem or prose-poem or versification or diversification for three
or four days: I'll never get all the weeds

out of the grass: I just know after each day that
there are a hell of a lot fewer weeds in the lawn:
it's evening: seven: I just noticed
a dark cloud coming from the west, so I went out

and said, please, rain some here: a few pin drops
fell, I think though more because of the dark cloud than the
saying: saying doesn't do any good but it doesn't
hurt: aligns the psychic forces with the natural:

that alignment may have some influence: I have found the world
so marvelous that nothing would surprise me: that may sound
contradictory, the wrong way to reach the matter-of-fact: but
if you can buy comets sizzling around in super-elongated

orbits and a mathematics risen in man that corresponds to the
orbits, why, simple as it is finally, you can move on to glutinous
molecules sloshing around in the fallen seas for something
to stick to: that there should have been possibilities enough to

include all that has occurred is beyond belief, an extreme the
strictures and disciplines of which prevent loose-flowing
phantasmagoria: last night in the cloud-darkened dusk rain began
gently, the air so full of moisture it just couldn't help it,

and continued at least past midnight when I went to bed: this
morning is dark but not raining: recovery's widespread: rain
comes all over everything: trees, bushes, beans, petunias,
weeds, grass, sandboxes, garages: yesterday I went with the hose

on the hard crusty ground from one single scorched patch to
another, never able to stay long at one point the other places
were calling so hard: ocean dumping of nuclear garbage requires
technological know-how, precision of intention, grace of

manipulation: devilish competition invades even the dirty work
of the world, where, though, the aggressive, intelligent young man
can negotiate spectacular levels of promotion: we have spilt
much energy generating concentrations—nerve gas, specific

insecticides, car polish, household cleansers "fatal if swallowed"—
we must depend on land, sea, and air to diffuse into harmlessness:
but some indestructibles resist all transformation and anyway
our vast moderators are limited: an oil slick covers every inch

of ocean surface: at the poles pilots see in the contrast the
sullied air's worldwide: because of the circulations, water can
never be picked up for use except from its usages, where what
has gone in is not measured or determined: extreme calls to

extreme and moderation is losing its quality, its effect: the
artificial has taken on the complication of the natural and where
to take hold, how to let go, perplexes individual action: ruin
and gloom are falling off the shoulders of progress: blue-green

globe, we have tripped your balance and gone into exaggerated
possession: this seems to me the last poem written to the world
before its freshness capsizes and sinks into the slush: the
rampaging industrialists, the chemical devisers and manipulators

are forging tanks, filling vats of smoky horrors because of
dollar lust, so as to live in long white houses on the summits
of lengthy slopes, for the pleasures of making others spur and
turn: but common air moves over the slopes, and common rain's

losing its heavenly clarity: if we move beyond
the natural cautions, we must pay the natural costs, our every
extreme played out: where we can't create the room of
playing out, we must avoid the extreme, disallow it: it's Sunday

morning accounts for such preachments, exhortations, and
solemnities: the cumulative vent of our primal energies is now and

always has been sufficient to blow us up: I have my ventilator
here, my interminable stanza, my lattice work that lets the world

breeze unobstructed through: we could use more such harmless
devices: sex is a circular closure, permitting spheric
circularity above hemispheric exchange: innocent, non-destructive,
illimitable (don't you wish it) vent: I want to close (I may

interminably do it, because a flatness is without beginning,
development, or end) with my chief concern: if contaminated
water forces me to the extreme purification of bottled or distilled
water, the extreme will be costly: bulldozers will have to clear

roads to the springs: trucks will have to muck the air to bring
the water down: bottles will have to be made from oil-fired
melts: a secondary level of filth created to escape the first:
in an enclosure like earth's there's no place to dump stuff off.

Mid-August

Now the ridge
brooks
are
flue-dry, the rocks

parching hot &
where sluice
used
to clear roots &

break weeds down brambly,
light finds a luminous
sand-scar,
vertical: it will

go to a hundred
today: even the
zucchini vine has
rolled over

on its
side.

Clearing the Dark Symbiosis

Any entangling however
scandent and weighty
is likely
if it's lasted some eons

to show mutuality, fervor
symbiotic, if
in the first trials
unravelingly scary:

for example, the hollyhocks
strung out tall,
the peaks heavy with
bud-nub and bloom sway,
I started to look out thinking

thunder, thunder-made or making
wind, would down
those highest blooms, or
rain and wind would: but

the morning glory vines,
taking over like sudden guests,
built a holding between
all the hollyhock stalks,
a mutual house, an air house:

the storm came, well you know,
but the vines were just

sufficient to keep the margin of
extremity off: I said
well in the fall (almost)
when the

hollyhock has very little
to lose, it has still itself
to gain: add, for me,
the morning glory blooms.

Viable

Motion's the dead give away,
eye catcher, the revealing risk:
the caterpillar sulls on the hot macadam

but then, risking, ripples to the bush:
the cricket, startled, leaps the
quickest arc: the earthworm, casting,

nudges a grassblade, and the sharp robin
strikes: sound's the other
announcement: the redbird lands in

an elm branch and tests the air with
cheeps for an answering, reassuring
cheep, for a motion already cleared:

survival organizes these means down to
tension, to enwrapped, twisting suasions:
every act or non-act enceinte with risk or

prize: why must the revelations be
sound and motion, the poet, too, moving and
saying through the scary opposites to death.

Precursors

In a little off-water
snaggy with roots

I dibbled

thinking
what a brand new place this is—
the surprising fauna,
scribblings
scribbling in water, landing

in mud-dust,
the spectacular green moss
creeping down
stump slopes to waterlevel,

and, look, clouds appear
in the ground
here, puddles
perfectly representational,
giving day or night
totally back:
it was so new

I thought I must've invented
it, or at least said it
first into the air:

but when I looked around
there were a thousand
puddles—had been
thousands more—some larger
than mine
in an over-place
called a swamp:

over-place led on to over-place
to the one place where
invisibility broke
out vacancy's flawless opacity:

but there, so the story
end good,

a turn brought me back

to this particular old
dawdling hole,

the wonders greener than they were,
the mirror clearer,
the fauna (and flora)
diverser, tangled,

the oldest things freshest,
most in need of being told.

Lonesome Valley

This time of year a bumblebee's
sometimes found off
well away from anywhere
with a ragged wing:

seems foreign, probably, to him,
once a smooth bullet shot clear over
untroubling shrubs,
the difficulty of giving
grass and tiny, spangling
clover leaves:

as if from anger, a very high blurred buzz
comes and the bee lofts
three inches off, falls one-sided,

perplexed in a perfect scramble
of concretion—

immense vines & stalks brushy
interweaving—

frost's the solution still
distant

but too much effort in the crippled
condition can
do it too

or being dragged down by ants,
the sucked dryness,
the glassy wings perfectly remnant
in their raggedness,
the body shell shellacked complete,
the excessive hollowness and lightness.

Delaware Water Gap

Rounding the mountain's rim-ledge,
we looked out valleyward
onto the summits of lesser hills,

summits bottoms of held air, still lesser
heights clefts and ravines: oh, I said,
the land's a slow ocean, the long blue

ridge a reared breakage, these small peaks
dips and rises: we're floating,
I said, intermediates of stone and air,

and nothing has slowed altogether
into determination and a new wave
to finish this one is building up somewhere,

a continent crowded loose, upwarping
against its suasions, we, you and I,
to be drowned, now so sustained and free.

Day

On a cold late
September morning,

wider than sky-wide
discs of lit-shale clouds

skim the hills,
crescents, chords
of sunlight
now and then fracturing

the long peripheries:
the crow flies
silent,
on course but destinationless,

floating:
hurry, hurry,
the running light says,
while anything remains.

Staking Claim

Look, look where the mind can go
I said to the sanctified
willows
wreathing jittery slow slopes of wind

look it can go up up to the ultimate
node where
remembering is foretelling
generation, closure
where taking in is giving out
ascent and descent a common blip

look going like wind over rocks
it can
touch where
completion is cancellation

all the way to the final vacant core
that brings

things together and turns them away

all the way away
to stirless bliss!

and the willows,
dream-wraiths song-turned,
bent in troops of unanimity,
never could waken
never could feel the rushing days

never could feel the cold
wind and rushing days
or thoroughly know
their leaves taking flight:

look I said to the willows
what the mind
can apprehend,

entire and perfect staying,
and yet face winter's
face coming over the hill

look I said to the leaves
breaking into flocks around me taking
my voice away
to the far side of the hill
and way beyond gusting down the long changes

The Eternal City

After the explosion or cataclysm, that big
display that does its work but then fails
out with destructions, one is left with the

pieces: at first, they don't look very valuable,
but nothing sizable remnant around for
gathering the senses on, one begins to take

an interest, to sort out, to consider closely
what will do and won't, matters having become
not only small but critical: bulbs may have been

uprooted: they should be eaten, if edible, or
got back in the ground: what used to be garages,
even the splinters, should be collected for

fires: some unusually deep holes or cleared
woods may be turned to water supplies or
sudden fields: ruinage is hardly ever a

pretty sight but it must when splendor goes
accept into itself piece by piece all the old
perfect human visions, all the old perfect loves.

The Shoreless Tide

The universe with its
universal principles
was out exact with concision—

but toying, idling—
again this morning: that
is, the lemon-yellow

lime-veined sugar maple
leaves were as in a
morning tide, full but

slow with the slowness
of huge presences, nicking
off the branches and

coming down points up, stem-end
first, centered and weighted,
but spiraling nicely,

a dance perfectly

abundant: I got excited,
the universe concentrated

on the small scope of
a fall, as if to
expend reserves of

spectacle on the doomed so
we might, I thought, consider
some well beyond all loss.

Grace Abounding
for E.C.

What is the misery in one that turns one with gladness
to the hedge strung lucid with ice: is it that one's
misery, penetrating there as sight, meets neither

welcome nor reprimand but finds nevertheless a picture
of itself sympathetic, held as the ice-blurred stems
increased: ah, what an abundance is in the universe

when one can go for gladness to the indifferent ghastly,
feel alliances where none may ever take: find one's
misery made clear, borne, as if also, by a hedge of ice.

Phase

These still days after frost have let down
the maple leaves in a straight compression
to the grass, a slight wobble from circular to

the east, as if sometime, probably at night, the
wind's moved that way—surely, nothing else
could have done it, really eliminating the *as*

if, although the *as if* can nearly stay since
the wind may have been a big, slow
one, imperceptible, but still angling

off the perpendicular the leaves' fall:
anyway, there was the green-ribbed, yellow,
flat-open reduction: I just now bagged it up.

Hibernaculum

I

A cud's a locus in time, a staying change, moving
but holding through motions timeless relations,
as of center to periphery, core-thought to consideration,

not especially, I'd say, goal-directed, more
a slime- and sublime-filled coasting, a repeating of
gently repeating motions, blissful slobber-spun webs:

today's paper says that rain falls on the desert and makes
it fertile: semen slips, jets, swims into wombs
and makes them bulge: therefore, there must be

2

a big penis above the clouds that spills the rain:
that is, I think, reasonable, which says something for
reason operating in fictions akilter: reason's no

better off than its ambience, and an ambience can't
alter frequently from its reason: (somewhere, though,
along the arm of a backwoods spiral, interchange

and adjustment with the environment are possible but
adjustment likely to be at the surprise of reason,
displeasure included: but then there has to be

3

protection against jolt-change: smashing alterations,
kind of cottonpicking conniptions, fail of impulse:)
the thunderbolt, another celestial phallus, though,

sterile, peels trees, explodes bushes, ravels roots,
melds sand into imitation lightning, spurry and branchy,
deep into the ground: that sort of thing is

not promising, so represents, as with Zeus, authority:
cussed superegomaniacal threat that gets from the outside
in, doing its dirty work bitterest closest to

4

pleasure's fundament: the better it feels, the bigger
the bludgeon: O merciful constructions that are so made,
do have mercy: the stuff is sweet, why crud it up

with crud: for every fructifying heavenly penis, such as
the rain penis, a ghastly one seres sand:
if there were any way to get around the universe, somebody

would've by now: history informs despair:
the lucky young, they don't know anybody's screwed
or perished before: just as well, too: although

5

screwing is nearly worth perishing, and, too, the two not
always concomitant: perhaps, co-terminous: but then the
penis is also (like the heavens) splitting and pleasuring:

while it's in, it is, afterall, commanding and will not,
just because somebody's edgy, withdraw: it will come
out only when it backs off from a puzzled loss or when

something truly spectacular appears, a shotgun or, more
accurately, roused maiden aunt: rhythms, speeding up,
build necessity into their programs: I see filigrees of

6

confabulation, curlicues, the salt walking-bush, ah, I see
aggregates of definition, plausible emergences, I see
reticulations of ambience: the days shorten down to a

gap in the night, winter, though gray and vague, not half
dubious enough: I see a sleet-filled sky's dry freeze:
I see diggings disheveled, bleak mounds, burnt openings:

what do I see: I see a world made, unmade, and made again
and I hear crying either way: I look to the ground for the
lost, the ground's lost: I see grime, just grime, grain,

7

grit, grist: the layers at thousand-year intervals
accumulate, reduce to beginnings: but I see the nightwatchman
at the cave's mouth, his eyes turned up in stunned amusement

to the constellations: from zero to zero we
pass through magnificence too shatterable: sight, touch,
inquiring tongue, water spinning into white threads over rocks:

I see the man moving boldly, staking his love on time, time
the slippery, the slick mound stragglers slide into the
everlasting encompassing waters from: not a drop of water

8

hasn't endured the salt-change of change: how
have the clouds kept fresh, the soil kept lively, its
milling microbes, how has the air, drawn into numberless

dyings kept clarity, breatheability: I see quiet lakes
and composed hills: I see the seasonal wash of
white and green: I am alarmed with acceptance: nothing

made right could have been made this way, and nothing
made otherwise could have been made right: nothing can
be made to make it right: we're given the works to

9

purchase nothing: the hardest training of the eye
against this loveliness, what can we make of holding so
to what we must give up, as if only in the act of giving

up can we know the magnificence, spent: what are we
here to learn: how to come into our estates before night
disinherits us: dear God (or whatever, if anything, is

merciful) give us our lives, then, the full possession,
before we give them back: I see the flood-child astir in the
surf, the clouds slowing and breaking into light:

10

what did he buy or sell: what is the meaning of loss
that never lived into gain: the mother, not far off,
flickers in a ditch to the minor winds: how far off

she is, past all touch and dream, the child huddled
snug into himself, his decomposition: how the dark
mind feeds on darkness, hungry for the inmost core: but

it is only darkness, empty, the hollow, the black, sucking
wind: this everyone knows: everyone turns away: light,
tendril, moon, water seize our attention, make us turn:

11

I think we are here to give back our possessions before
they are taken away: with deliberate mind to say to
the crushing love, I am aware you are here cloaked in

this moment, you are priceless, eternity is between us,
we offer ourselves in the sacrifice of time to this
moment become unconditioned and time-evering: I think

we are here to draw the furthest tailing of time round
into the perishing of this purest instant: to make out
the proximity of love to a hundred percent and to zero:

12

I see the bitterest acquiescence, the calm eye in the
tragic scene, the smile of the howling mind: I keep
forgetting—I am not to be saved: I keep forgetting this

translation from fleshbody to wordbody is leaving my
flesh behind, that I *have* entered into the wordbody but
may not enter in, not at last: I need a set of practices,

a mnemonics, my fleshbody can keep close to its going:
of those practices the stepping out into love, motion's
glimpse, blanches to the highest burn: I can lose myself:

13

I'm not so certain I can lose you, I'm not so certain
you can lose me: but all the others have succeeded, all
the others have tricked on their legs by graves, all

the others have gotten through all the losses and left
the air clear, the bush aleaf, the ground in scent:
after it takes place, there will be a clearing for us,

too, we will be in the wind what shape a leaf would take
if a leaf were there: let's join to the deepest slowing,
turn the deepest dark into touch, gape, pumping, at the

14

dark beyond reach: afterwards, shoveling the driveway,
warming up the coffee, going to the grocery store, opening
the cookie jar, washing, shaving, vacuuming, looking out

the window at the perilously afflicted, that is, snow-loaded
bent evergreens, watching the pheasants walking across
the yard, plopping up belly-deep in snow, wondering

if one can get the car out or, out, in: the Ceremony of
Puzzling over the Typewriter, of swishing off the dishes
and getting them in the washer, of taking out the trash

15

and hearing the trash-can lids snap and bang, opened or
squeezed shut: the considerable distance the universe
allows between brushing the teeth and helping John put

his fort together: these small actions near the center
form the integrations, the gestures and melodies, rises
and falls minutes give over to hours, hours to days, days

to weeks, months, and years: it all adds up to zero only
because each filled day is shut away, vanished: and what
memory keeps it keeps in a lost paradise: the heroic

16

entangler, benign arachnid, casting threads to catch,
hang and snatch, draw up the filamental clutch, the
clump-core reticulate, to tie energy into verbal knots

so that only with the death of language dies the energy!
so all the unravellers may feed! the dissipators go with
some grain to their swill: pleasure to my tribe and

sufficient honor! to lean belief the lean word comes,
each scope adjusted to the plausible: to the heart
emptied of, by elimination, the world, comes the small

17

cry domesticating the night: if the night is to be
habitable, if dawn is to come out of it, if day is ever
to grow brilliant on delivered populations, the word

must have its way by the brook, lie out cold all night
along the snow limb, spell by yearning's wilted weed till
the wilted weed rises, know the patience and smallness

of stones: I address the empty place where the god
that has been deposed lived: it is the godhead: the
yearnings that have been addressed to it bear antiquity's

18

sanction: for the god is ever re-created as
emptiness, till force and ritual fill up and strangle
his life, and then he must be born empty again:

accost the emptiness saying let all men turn their
eyes to the emptiness that allows adoration's life:
that is my whole saying, though I have no intention to

stop talking: our immediate staying's the rock but
the staying of the rock's motion: motion, that spirit!
we could veer into, dimpling, the sun or into the cold

19

orbital lofts, but our motion, our weight, our speed
are organized here like a rock, our spiritual stay:
the blue spruce's become ponderous with snow: brief

melt re-froze and knitted ice to needles and ice
to snow so the ridges eight inches high hold: the
branches move back and forth, stiff wailers:

the cloud-misty moonlight fills small fields, plots,
woodnooks with high light, snow transluminant as
fire: the owl, I'll bet, looks about little from

20

those branchy margins, his eye cleaned of liking in
the soft waste not a mouse burrows or thrashes through,
liking gone inward and sharp into the agony of imagined

mouseful lands: one thing poetry could be resembled to is
soup: the high moving into clarity of quintessential
consomme: then broth, the homogeneous cast of substance's

shadow: then the falling out of diversity into specific
identity, carrot cube, pea, rice grain: then the chunky
predominance of beef hunk, long bean, in heavy gravy:

21

last night the eaves from roof heat dripped and the
drops in those close-holding freezing laminations
noded the tips of the cedar lobes hammer heavy, such

ice: today, though, some sunshine and in the mid-forties,
the freeing up has been steady, if slow: the blue
spruce stands isolated out in the yard—nothing drips

on it except the sky—and since mid-morning it has
had a little melt-shower in it, a shower canopy:
from a low-hung dangle the emptied branches have risen

22

to near horizontal and the snow left looks edged and
drained: I think in the marked up annals of recorded
evolutionary history mind will turn out to have been

nova-like, say; a pressure of chance built up
nature had to take, the slide toward the slow explosion
of searching risk: some think mind will continue

growing out of nature until possessed of its own self
second-nature it will bespeak its own change, turn with
or against the loam out of which it grew: I'm pessimistic:

23

for my little faith, such as it is, is that mind and
nature grew out of a common node and so must obey common
motions, so that dickering with second-nature mind

violates the violation: a made mind can live compre-
hendingly only in a made world and artifice, exact and
independent as it looks, can't, I'll bet, extend intricacy

working out through the core of every single atom: I
depend on the brook to look out where it's going:
I depend on the snow to ornament the woods: I depend

24

on the sun to get up every morning rightfully off-time:
I depend on the sea current to find just which way to
sway to the thermodynamic necessity: I depend utterly

on my body to produce me, keep me produced, don't you:
the autonomy of the mind! who could desire it, staying
up all night to keep the liver right, the pancreas calm:

I prefer like the sweet brook to be at ease with my
findings: I prefer the strictures that release me into
motion: for not even the highest branch is free to wave,

25

it responds as freedom to the wind's tyranny: what have
I to desire of autonomy except slavery, its ware:
I prefer to be offered up by all the designs and musculatures

into the liberty of correspondent motions: when the
mind can sustain itself it then may consider sustaining
the universe: meanwhile, I have nothing, nothing to sell:

I write what is left to write after everything's sold out:
and also I write not very wide, just to the fence or hedge
around the lot (sometimes from my window I take in the

26

neighboring lady's scrap of woods—I hope she
doesn't get word and charge me) but of course I write
straight up and down as far either way as I can reach,

which by sight (but not reach) one way is far but by
reach the other way, the ground, is near, if so opaque
only imagination, that frail, filters through: still

it's world enough to take my time, stretch my reason, hinder
and free me: do a section on the garage roof snow and you
will find several strata: I haven't looked but I know

27

because I was here when they happened: fluff snow, grit
snow, plain sleet, fluff snow, wet snow, more grit, and
snow (regular): similar sedimentary phenomena might be

expected elsewhere: and I have sat here by the window today
and seen a direct relation between the sunny intervals and
the rate of eave-melt off the garage: that close a

pull between the sun and my garage snow stuns me,
though I would be the last to insist it do a thing for you:
I really do not want to convince anyone of anything except

28

that conviction is cut loose, adrift and aswim, upon the
cool (sometimes sweltering) tides of roiling energy:
that's not to despise conviction, definition, or other

structure but to put them in their place: I hope
you are in the middle income bracket (at least): I
desire to be in the very high upper high outgo bracket:

to furnish forth energy out of nothing, except reflection,
a few hard years, several procedures of terror and
astonishment, New Hope Elementary School, assorted

29

mothers and fathers (with the one and the one), fifty
acres of ground, half swamp, half hill, Whiteville High
School, the Pacific Ocean, a small sweep through the arc

of the galaxy, one arm of the spiral in particular,
etc.: I know I can't give all that back but so what I
haven't quit trying yet and anyway it's just giving

nothing to nothing: I'm somewhat shocked by clouds
of organic compounds in deep space but anticipate
no flagrant reaction: I think it's going to rain:

30

our young don't believe in time as future and, so,
suffer every instant's death: they don't believe
in the thread, plot, the leading of one thing into

another, consequence, developed change: without retrospect
or prospect, they seek the quality of experience
a moment's dimension allows: thrill replaces

goal: threat lessens and fractures time, shortening
the distance to the abyss, immediate, a step away:
without calm, they can't see tomorrow unfolding: the mind,

31

too, can't move beyond the surface event into the
assimilations of higher, restful suasions where arc-like
staying has beginning and end and smooth curvature

reliable: hell is the meaninglessness of stringing out
events in unrelated, undirected sequences: remove danger
(holocaust, suffocation, poisoning) from the young and

their anxieties will unwind into long reaches of easeful
seeking: not that anyone is, has been, or ever will be
more than a hair away from disaster, and the statistics

32

on anyone's living forever are unpromising: still,
we have now a Myth of Disaster, and that's harder than
some other kinds of myth: with another snow coming, we

drove out past Route 13 on North Hanshaw this afternoon
to the tree farm for a scotch pine: there was half an
acre of perfectly spaced trees tied up to permanent

stakes: that was enough, some of the stakes deserted:
nevertheless, I bought a full, short, four-dollar tree
which I've just put twinkle lights on: now, with

33

the snow still steady, John and Robbie (his little
friend) are doing their part, hanging balls and
icicles: christmas is still five days away, but no

matter—anticipation starts to burst out of little boys
early, and a present to raising the tree must be opened:
vent, vent: we need every trigger and valve we can

invent to achieve restless deflations: invent vents:
my enormous, airy self sputters like a balloon at its
inadequate outlet and shoots off spinning enlarging circles

34

into the galaxy—or at least over the fence and treetops or
halfway over the lake: when it gets too dry around here
in the summer sometimes, the little creeks nearly creak

with drought, a dribble of a drop dropping off the
dry ledges: well, I could use a little of that spareness
of form and volume: imagine the luxurious lassitude of

taking five minutes to swell into a drop and then let
go with a lengthy reluctance: the last drop bulbing
from the spent member: but little boys have small

35

emotional bladders and the pressure's terrific: they'd
rather have a string of little wow's every day
than build up to one big blast: I see the gully-wash,

lineated at the bottom with every stone the flash
could reach and roll into marcation: the honeybee sings
by the hard cactus, wings, spines, works his way up to

the barrel-tip blossom wet, resilient with the roothair
aperture of giving: somewhere in a dry trunk, the grog-rich
honey cushioning the beeswax: I see the industry of water

36

variously dense and laden, the distributions, the little
pools, saved lockets: the bead in the ant belly,
the thread in a cactus vein, the reservoirs of birds'

eyes: the droplet concentrations: I keep thinking
I'm saved, a shock of mild hilarity! I keep thinking
I'm a pot eternity is dropping coins in! think,

if you will, of that: or I keep thinking these words
translate me into another body less affected by
the weather and time's clicking subtractions:

37

public, I have nothing to say to you, nothing: except,
look at the caterpillar under this clump of grass: it
is fuzzy: look at the sunset: it is colorful: listen:

it's hard to compete here in winter: snow makes the
broadest impression, an ineradicable eradication: slows
and muffles: you can hear the snow fall, a fizz: if

I cannot look at you, I can look with you: since there
is something between us, let it be a thing we share:
if there is nothing between us, I'm coming up with this:

38

by the time I got the world cut down small enough that
I could be the center of it, it wasn't worth having:
but when I gave up center, I found I was peripherally

no bigger than a bit: now, I have decided the former
was the better: I must re-mount the center and force
the world to subside about me: not easy and not

promising, but neither is surrender: still, St. Francis
said if you give up everything it's all yours: giving
up is not easy at all: why is everything so perplexing:

39

I feel in the company of the soul, however, nervous:
I grow arch and curt: I talk nasty: I wink and grunt or
switch to salacity: I mouth reprovables: I don't

belong here, I try to announce: I am not worthy: I say
to the soul, you know this is no place for me: I am,
besides impolite, flawed: but the soul absorbs my defense

and turns my pain into a pure form of itself, investing
my embarrassment with grace: I go out to the hedge bush-vine,
but there is the soul, tangled with curvature: I look at

40

the gaunt maple, but a nest is hung in it: I look
at the points of the picket fence, but there, too, the
snowflakes hold: in between, thinner than sight,

returns and compliances give and take: can I take this
in, I ask, stand with it, assume it: can I talk of it just
as it stalls against the garage, bends upward and outward

around the eaves, picks up a drift and walks it to the edge:
is there an accepting it so complete it vanishes, my wills
and motions tidings in a tide: ah, soul, I say,

41

awkwardness is being conscious of you: I will move and
do directly as I like and that way correspond to your
liking: the point is just to get this page full so I can

take it out of the typewriter and write some letters: sour
cream, yogurt, cottage cheese, chip dip: lizard,
lick-flicking: rancher, ranching: fly, buzzing: tiger,

hassling: cicada, burr-grinding: squirrel, leaping:
chicken, walking: fur, flying: day, breaking: dove,
alighting: fish, gulping: sight, seeing: nose, running:

42

a poem variable as a dying man, willing to try anything,
or a living man, with the consistency of either direction:
just what the mind offers to itself, bread or stone:

in the swim and genesis of the underlying reality things
assume metes and bounds, survive through the wear
of free-being against flux, then break down to swim and

genesis again: that's the main motion but several
interturns have been concocted to confuse it: for example,
the human self risks chaos by breaking down to a flash of

43

single cells in order to plant the full human code early
in the beginning: and many other continuities of pattern,
as slowed flux, work through the flux durably: adagio

in furioso: a slow bass line to a treble revel: tell
him he is lost, he will turn in there and show you what
lost is, a positive sight: tell him his iciness is perfect,

he will lower the cold till perfection drifts like sleep
to aimless absoluteness: tell him he is thin, he will
become so thin the spiritual will take charge: he will

44

turn into any failure abruptly as into a detour and find
his way to a highway: tell him he knows beauty,
he will, going and trying, disclose ugliness: virtue is

waiting anywhere to be by concision of dealing established:
chiefly in the virtueless: huntsman, huntsman, how many
hounds arunning: a lead-hound and a following:

breaking, moving, and filling: people who dress up like
artists, their art form is dressing up like artists:
the sun came up this morning without clouds before it:

45

what is it, then, that the poem is trying to give us
an image of: the ideal image of the ideal man: invariably:
the realist wants to know ideally the ideal realist: the

ragged man and the ragged poem aspire to ideal raggedness:
the loose or fragmented or scopy: the mind can't conceive
any way except into the desired image, the ideal, that's

the only way it works right: let there be, he said
prayerfully though he was only talking, more mass and less
direction, so that the propaganda cannot get off the pad

46

and the concision cannot gather to incision and the
over-simplification cannot settle real clear, accumulative
diversity a dreadnought bristling stifled guns: let

there be, he continued, orb-gathered complication, fuzzy,
bewildering, so that right carries a heavy bilge of wrong
and wrong looks as if it could sump out right: let—

he moved to the rostrum—certainly wallow iceberg-deep in
confusion: let nobody know very much precisely about
anything in—here, puzzled, he dozed: take that lady:

47

her mind is always lying down pleasing the legions: it is
a bow leant in a corner, gaunt with decommission:
how long did that last last last: it's snowing now with

the sun shining: squalls with clearings: today is Tues-
day: yesterday there were 9 hrs and 2 minutes of
daylight, sunup to sundown: that means light is

broadening: right here at the edge of winter-beginning's
winter-ending: today will probably be 9 hrs and 3 minutes:
tomorrow will be different, maybe 9 hrs and 4 minutes:

48

what is the prevailing tone: are there minutes of the
last meeting: should articles be padded with dummy
footnotes: are there any concepts to circulate: can

anyone form a motion: if we stall, will we sink:
if we run, will thinness split underfoot: the mind's
one: it pre-existed, I think: even before it was

mind it was mind plausible: it was the earth: when
it is fully born, it will be another earth, just like
the earth, but visionary, earth luminous with sight:

49

it will be nearly half dark: contemplation dwells on
one thing at a time: it will have lows and highs,
basins and high countries, peaks and abysses, naked

seabottoms and naked summits: it will have interior
circulations, crusts in slow flotation: the wind
will blow through it and rock will confront it: it

will be oriented to polar transactions: nothing will
be left out, nothing, not a thing, and yet it will be
whole: there will be islands, island chains, bays,

50

peninsulas, bottom spreads, inland seas, and mind will
have below its active surface several layers of
sedimentary history, though below that will be the

melts in high heat and heavy pressure, the mobility
underlying encrustation and phenomenological flux:
there is one mind and one earth: it was all there

before it was first discovered and nothing will have
been added when it is fully elaborated: and yet it is
completely unknown until made out: then the cosmos:

51

why does he write poems: it's the only way he can mean
what he says: you mean, say what he means: yes,
but it's harder for him to mean something than say

something: his sayings are facile, light-headed, and
discontinuous: he keeps saying in order to hope he will
say something he means: poems help him mean what he says:

poems connect the threads between the tuft of his head
and the true water: that's important to him, like roots
to a turf: without it, the separation would be awful:

52

poems deepen his attention till what he is thinking
catches the energy of a deep rhythm: then he becomes
essentially one: one in thought and motion: then, he

means: the recent forward brain is working with the
medulla oblongata: by the time I get to the end of this
all, I'll have to have found something to say to the

people: this scratching around in the private self has
to yield something beyond a private waste of time: I
have to say, here is my drop of glue, now, somebody,

53

hold the world together, or just yourself: I have to say,
here is a saying, binding: I must not when I get up on
the soapbox wash out: here, I will say, is my offering

to the people, these few words right at the center of my
experience of me and you: the complicated, elaborate weaving
of interconnection: I want to do well: I want people to say,

did you hear that, that sounded good: perhaps I will say,
the cosmos, as I understand it, wants you to have fun:
or I will say, your deepest error may be divine:

54

much have I studied, trashcanology, cheesespreadology,
laboratorydoorology, and become much enlightened and
dismayed: have, sad to some, come to care as much for

a fluted trashcan as a fluted Roman column: flutes are
flutes and the matter is a mere substance design takes
its shape in: take any subject, everything gathers up

around it: friend of mine is studying barbedwireology
and he finds you can marshal up much world and history
around the discipline: barbedwire limitations and

55

intellectual definitions produce about the same
securities and disasters: I think a lot about meter and
right away it becomes the mirror in which I see the face

of the times: oh, but the hierarchy of subjects persists,
sociology way above scabology, philosophy a sight beyond
toothbrushosophy: the aristocracy of learning is so much

will: I'd as soon know one thing as another, what's the
difference, it all fits and comes out the same: and I
can tell you, I'd rather see a tempest in a teapot

56

than Shakespeare plain: but Shakespeare was all right:
a nursemaid's lip meant as much to him as the king's eye:
but he never got it straight that in talking about the

actual king and the symbolical king he was merely
engaging a problem in rhetoric: well, I'm glad because
I can't reconcile the one with the many either—except

in the fuzzy land of radiant talk—and if Shakespeare grossly
surpassing me failed, I don't have to worry about surpassing
others, my place comfortable in the lowerarchy:

57

work's never done: the difficult work of dying
remains, remains, and remains: a brain lobe squdging
against the skull, a soggy kidney, a little vessel

smartly plugged: wrestling with one—or those—until
the far-feared quietus comes bulby, floating, glimmer-wobbling
to pop: so much more mechanical, physical than

spiritual-seeming grief: than survivors' nights filled
without touch or word, than any dignity true for a state
of being: I won't work today: love, be my leisure:

58

there is something dwelling in too correspondent for
haphazardry: I read Plotinus once, a little, and
saw my mind (increased): currents, polar fads,

flash back and forth through a center apparently staid:
we may just now be getting enough lead into time to note
that nothing at all is moving except into the halfways

of diversion: what if at the core the final eye's
design's fixed, the vision beaming locked, we the motes
crossing about, breaking into and dropping out

59

of light: what if we're not seeking the light at all,
the transfixion (stare to stare in a bereft learning)
but worrying the corners of our confined, held

suasions for the exit we could, from the starved light,
choose: why has the dark taken so much if darkness is
not the satisfaction: and how have we found the will

to thrive through the light from sway to sway: O
Plotinus (Emerson, even) I'm just as scared as comforted
by the continuity, one sun spelling in our sun-made heads:

60

I exist by just so much as I am will-lessly borne
along: I am as given up as the boat-sloped maple leaf
on fast water: not a thing remains, not a motion's

curl, of any desire, and none of the things I desired
and gathered are with me: I deserve nothing, not
a glimpse into this world overbearingly rich, this

hungry, hardly-visionable air: just as empty as I am
is the just emptiness, not a leaf between here and
extinction I have not spent the night in luminous

61

supplication with: by just so much as a tide flows in
and lifts me floating, by just so much I can never
grin the deathgrin at the silver abundance until I must:

where I never came to self, repletion's an abundant
wind (I'm picking out the grains, gritty, between me
and that abundance): considerable as any least

burdockflower, I'm alive to the stalk tip: anything
cries salvation big as capturing a waterfall: by just
so much as I have given up, I am sustained till finally

62

the boat bumps solid, sucks the surface tit, and, bloated, drowns:
today's the first of the year, icicle, cloud, root
in a slow procedure, every house re-roofed with snow:

the biggest numbers represent the finest differences:
plus or minus two parts of variation in a trillion, as
in narrowing down on the inconstant readings of a

fundamental constant—the mass of the electron, the
speed of light, or the hyperfine splitting in hydrogen
proton precessions: nature seems firm with casual

63

certainties (one could say a steel spike is a foot
long) but pressed for certainty breaks out
in bafflings of variability, a thousand close

measurings of the spike averaged out and a thousand
efforts to average out the variables in the instruments
of measure or in the measuring environment

(room temperature, humidity, the probable frequency
the door to the room is opened): recalcitrance is built
in perfectly, variations thereon perceived as possibility:

64

oh, I'm going to walk right out onto th'elision fields,
eat up gloria in the morning and have it out with her
in the evening: I'm going to postpone reality (but for

cheeseburgers) and focus yearning, doubly focus it,
bring into view three-dimensional hopes and hokum:
dying here sour with flesh and sweat—the disposition

of nature's bounty, a bounteous abandonment to sludge,
desireless, breathless: otherwise, otherwise to the limit!
if all must come down, make a high possibility for the

65

dependable work, space out an extreme differential,
an illusion for the future: the poet entangles: the
critic untangles: the poet, baited by illusion, figures

that massive tangling will give locus to core-tangles
and core-tangles to *the* core-tangle that will
fix reality in staid complication, at that central

core's center the primordial egg of truth: ah, what an
illusion: from the undifferentiated core-serum the mind
turns back to the definition of its tangles for rescue

66

and then back to the core for clarification, only to
hesitate in quandary's puzzlement: carefully, the critic
unwinds thread from thread, making out the energy and

translating it into ratiocination: but the untangling
done, all the untangling done, nothing remains but the
dumb end of the last thread and the opus of statement

that replaces it: illusion! illusion! there are not
two somethings but two nothings: one nothing surrounds,
extends beyond, the fullest entanglement, and the other

67

nothing is an infinitesimal dot of void at the center of
the primordial egg: inside calls to outside: in between
is the choice, an impoverishment that does away even with

the egg, or an abundance of entanglement very much like
the world but also nothing: for myself, I would rather
wear beads than have no neck at all: the void is the

birthplace of finches, gyrfalcons, juncos (a specialty),
snowy egrets, woodcocks, hummingbirds, crows, jays,
wood ducks, warblers, titmice, and the end of everything:

68

I dreamed Edna St. Vincent Millay's female companion
had just arrived on the beach of Europe and was reciting
a moving poem about why had they come back when their old

friends had resettled or were lying in the sod: it was
a very sad poem and the lady was sad and wrinkled:
I woke up just before crying myself, impressed with

the power of the poetry and life's risky changes:
the morning was cloudless, rosy with atmosphere, the sun
already brightened to appear suddenly over the sudden ridge:

69

a little philosophy never hurt anybody: or else, little
philosophy hurts everybody: takes a lot of philosophy to
make a little philosopher: the bubble swells and bursts,

the leavings cherishable, as being of themselves, not
devoted to an organ of use but, as with balloons, dumbly
elastic, shrunk wrinkled, and, often, highly colorful:

constituting an encounter of thing to thing: the bubble
bursts and then one participates in the universal energy
of biting an apple, having a tooth filled, turning a

70

corner (the friction and earth-displacement of that) so
that the universe seems available in the
gravity of a ladybug tipped down a blade of grass:

there's a difference between division and differentiation:
from the primal energy, much has split away into identity—
toothpicks, yew berries, jungle gyms, pole beans (the

thoughtful differentiations into bell pepper and basil)—
but a little time undercuts these matters into shape (soon
they will be shapelessly available again) so that division

71

is, at most, temporal—(mind & body) ha! (mind & nature) ha!
(reality & appearance) ha! (dream & fact) ha!—no, no, this
is not an expression of division, of taxonomy, dogma, bouncy

triadic motion, structure, solidification, type, but of
identity differentiation: one of the strongest thrusts,
you might say, is to perish away from unity the fully

discrete, expressed, captured hollybush—the lust to
individuation we've heard so much about: let me, the cry
is, stand like the drop cast back from the breaking

72

crest apart and regard the other satisfactory expressions
so there may be action, interaction, contrariety, and sum:
but the rise into differentiation is exactly equal

to the fall, a just compact not too friendly to the
appetite ravingly incomplete, or something, the deflections
into limbo: routes go awry but everything anyhow gets

safely, if reluctantly, back into circulation, the
least differentiae nearest the continuum: it's true the
splits sometimes look perfect, the divisions ghastly, severe

73

alienation an agreeing merely with temporality: but actually
while the leaf may not answer one's questions, it waves, a
nice language, expressive and complete: and if the ladybug,

traveling across the droppy peaks of grass, seems not my friend,
then I have not understood hanging to cool in shade; or
legs nimbly feeling for grass-hair; or any other

sight-loud talk: if I pick a leaf, it wilts: if I cap a
spring, it swells: if I crush a grass-spear, it stains:
if the quince crowds the hollyhock, the hollyhock

74

bends away, suffering subtle losses of rectitude:
what am I to say: my brotherhood's immense, and if the gods
have vanished that were never here I do not miss them:

some universe comes here to my yard every day or so and bursts
into a fly standing, with six little dents, on water: sometimes
when I'm shaving, a real small fly, screen-penetrating, gets

stuck in a bowl-drop of water: but he wiggles and would be all
right if something could be done with the whole him, floating:
but when I touch a tissue to the drop of water, tension pulls him

75

down, crushing him limp, so he never gets up, no matter how
dry: a killing rescue: some things will not work: one day
I poured brine and salt-ice from the icecream freezer onto

a strip of ground near the hedge: earthworms walloped up
rampant and thrashing and then went puffy-limp and
white: I have killed I can't tell how many thousand priceless

moths and flies (even goldfinches and bright-streaked warblers)
sucked up by the grill or radiator grid: all of these lives
had been acting in accordance with given principles, identical

76

to my own: nothing's changed, with all the divisions
and terrors: the physical drowns and buoys, divides and comes
together: the bird's song-air's in my range, comes on my air:

I wrote the foregoing passage in July last year, which accounts
for the change of weather and some summery tone: and a
slightly longer line: winter is different, shortening:

if you believe in equivocation as a way then you
must also believe in univocation because that is one
of the possibilities of equivocation: and if you

77

believe all is fire why then everything is, including
the stones' dull music, solid, slow, and
cold: and the weatherless moon less is nevertheless

singing blips of meteoric bits, the flash
smirching to glistening moon-tears of solar effusions,
the wind, the solar wind, that pours out coronal lacings

into a great space: and then the mud by the swamp
ponds with cloud trails of crawdads scurrying is working
with little cellular thrivings: and the cool fire of

78

ferns climbing tree-footings from the deep freshets:
allow, allow for the cryogenic event even, low down
nearly where the atoms give up relation and drift in slow

falls, incredible, spaceless beads: that is an extreme
form of burning, say, but of the fire: I can't
help thinking that what we have is right enough, the

core of the galaxy, for example, a high condition,
ample, but here, though, on the surface at least,
toads, picnic tables, morning glories, firs afire:

79

the world seems to me a show closed down, a circus
left standing: the ropes slack, the loose tent
bellies and whomps in the wind like a scared gigantic

jellyfish: some stragglers are around but they are
turned inward on their purposelessness: they make up
directions that go nowhere: they turn missing corners:

the clown's paint has worn off: his rags have become
rags: his half-bald wig has become his head, his falls
have become his tricks: he now clowns to the universe:

80

now meter is interesting: the prospects are before
us: I feel the need for a realistic approach: we were
promised for today nine hours and six minutes of

daylight: we were promised no sunlight and received
none: but can you imagine forty degrees: we have it:
the ground is practically asplatter with eavesdropping:

there are pools under the floating mush: they are not
clearly of a depth: one must know the terrain well or
fill his boots: the garage, the cold garage, and the

81

porch still have six inches of snow but the house across
the way whose second floor is all under a slanting roof
is snow-free: the woods, unhung completely,

have resumed an old darkness, whereas yesterday they were
still irradiated with snowholdings: the sun,
invisible before, has set into another invisibility and

the consequences are darkening here through the clouds:
oh this little time-drenched world! how it jiggles with
flickering! light as history, as relic, light two

82

billion years old, moves its ancient telling through
the universe and deposits right here on my grass on a
clear night dim sediment of sizable duration: that

light can be so old and far-traveled, like flint, no
prayerstone that constant, the permanent telling of
that quickness: lucky that only by the equalizing instant

anything survives, lucky for us, who can thereby kiss
out time to a full reduction and know everything ravished,
burnt out in a lid's quickness: the total second:

83

sir, I told him, you have so many tones I can't tell
which one's prevailing: the dominant from the
predominant: you have so many, they come in chords,

tonic, subdominant, diminished: I can't tell the
significant significances from the insignificant
significances: won't you, I implored, thin out your

registration or, at least, give discernible direction
to your componency: it would take a battery of tonometers
just to find out about where you're at: in the

84

contextual sense: have something to say: say it:
need you spray sense and be trusted only in the spray's
shape: such enlargements of limitation often

fail into disorientation at the center: boo boo pee
doo: plot a course, Mr. Sulu: let's split: poetic
action mirrors human action: what preserves the

absurdist through the enactment of absurdity, what but
the feathery need to touch ideal absurdity: the
ideal's an imperishable validity: the illumination

85

identity takes thrust toward: it is the proposition
how we are to live our lives: the ideal hero and the
ideal anti-hero have ideality in common: heroes may

change ways, clothes, directions, moods, but all bear
the pressure of ideality: James, the train robber,
sublime: Appleseed, the life of service, yes:

the vacuum cleaner salesman can, in our time, hardly
give the imagination suction, gather dust into any
credible bag: rail splitter, spike driver, done, gone:

86

the sum of everything's nothing: very nice: that
turns the world back in on itself: such as right
when you possess everything, you'd give everything

up for a sickle pear: I hope my philosophy will turn
out all right and turn out to be a philosophy so as
to free people (any who are trapped, as I have been)

from seeking any image in the absolute or seeking
any absolute whatsoever except nothingness:
nothingness, far from being failure's puzzlement,

87

is really the point of lovely liberation, when
gloriously every object in and on earth becomes just
itself, total and marvelous in its exact scope,

able to exist without compromise out to the precise
skin-limit of itself: it allows freedom to fall
back from the thrust to the absolute into the world

so manifold with things and beings: the hollyhock,
what a marvel, complete in itself: the bee,
how particular, how nothingness lets him buzz

88

around: carless in Gaza, with a rocker arm on a valve
snapped, I to the gas station made it this morning,
left car, and by taxi so-forthed with son and wife

to University, son and wife going on beyond me to
nursery school: lunch hour nearing, I decided to
hitchhike home and did, first with a lady and baby

daughter all in a foreign small car, then with two
toughlooking guys from Virginia, leaned front seat
forward and let me in the back: we talked about

89

the snow, local squalls filling the air even though
the sun was shining: the driver said he had to get
back to Pennsylvania this afternoon: I asked if he had

snowtires and he said, No, and said he'd heard he could
get picked up if he got stuck without snowtires:
whereupon, apprehensively bound to be cheerful and useful,

I said when it's so cold like today the roads
stay dry even with the snow because the cars blow the
snow away as if it were feathers and that probably

90

he wouldn't have any trouble: just then a dog glanced
out onto the road, the driver, pushing back in his
seat, soaked on the brakes, and the car slid hardly at

all, verifying, as if by a universal complicity, my
faith's predictions: well, then, as we neared the
Corners, things seemed with me a little brighter, so

I said, that stop sign ahead would be perfect for me:
he would have to stop anyway, and I would know
immediately, if the other guy didn't open the door, that

91

I was about to be robbed, killed, or bent out of my will
which seemed about the worst thing: all went well,
ruining the story: I got out, saying thankyous and

wishingwells and walked about the mile down Hanshaw
home: just turning the curve in sight of home, I saw,
as in a perfect vision, my wife and son pulling up into

the driveway, driven back from nursery school in someone's
luminous stationwagon: I felt relieved: I said, ah, the
broken and divergent lines of morning are coalescing:

92

Wilde in some ways *contra naturam* really was: he loved
Art and set it against Nature, possibly because Art is
overwhelmed by Nature and he identified with being

overwhelmed: somewhat *contra mundum*, too: since
social nature had a majority against him: well, he did
rather well, a sort of terrier of the mind: he barked,

if mostly in the regions where opposites are clear, not
reconciled: I admire that: why think nature good if it's
against you: if it's against you, then it's hard to

93

approve even what produced you: not to approve what
produced you, though, bumfuzzles, since it's a kind
of suicidal vindication to hate nature in order to

love the self: how twisty things are: nature ought to
bear the blame, then, for fumbling, or society
learn to approve nature even when it fumbles, as being

also nature: well, I don't know what to hope in that
way, since society is also *contra naturam*, a device, a
convention: but if so how could Wilde come to love

94

convention so, I mean, convention as artifice, not the
conventional: Wilde, Art, Society, Convention—and then
convention damned him: that shuts off most of the roads

and suggests not detours but deadends: when a lioness
whelps a defective cub, she whomps it against the
ground till it's dead: well, I think we ought to put

ourselves above the beasts and take care to be respectful
where persons move: provided all persons move with
respect: we should exhaust all our virtues, first:

95

though it's gooseegg zero, morning sunlight hits the
strip of woods broadside and a squirrel is sitting out
pretty still on a limb taking in the direct radiation:

enormous jungle-like fronds of ice (and other configurations
like species) have run across possessing the outer windows
but, now, the sun up, thaw like a fungus is making dark

melts in the foliage: the sun's arc rises a little
daily into the world, marking a slightly longer
journey along the ridge between rising and setting:

96

yesterday afternoon, right after I had written about
the adventures of the morning, the gas station called and
said my car was ready: I had been thinking how many

days, not how many hours, it would take: so John, that's
his name up at Ned's Corners Station, drove the car on
down here to 606, less than a mile, and I made out a

check for him ($19.39), dropped him back at the station,
and took off for the University, free and mobilized again!
the total parts came to $7.79, 1 push rod ($1.25), 1

97

rocker arm ($1.35), 1 rocker retainer ($0.50), 1 set 2
gaskets @ $2.10 ($4.20), and 1 roll electrical tape ($0.49):
the total labor was $10.50: r & r (remove and repair?)

l. (left?) valve cover, r & r both valve covers, replace
rocker arm, push rod, & retainer on #4 cyl intake valve:
all in all I thought I got off easy: one thing interesting

is that Ned's Corners Station is at 909 Hanshaw Road
and I'm 606 Hanshaw Road: that's configuration:
today is, as I said, bright and cold: but 9 hrs 12 min.:

98

everyday (somedays, twice) I remember who I am and I
metamorphose away through several distracting transformations
till I get myself out in bidable shape on comfortable

ground, and then the shows, the transactions, carry
traces of such brilliant energy of invention that I am
half willing to admire my new self, thrust into its

lofty double helices, so winding: well, that's one way
to get out of the dumps, but they say it's wiser to
find the brilliants right in the dumps themselves: but on

99

the show side, there's not only the show itself, bodiless
if arresting, but the honest mechanisms that produced
the show: those mechanisms are earnest and work to

conserve their energy through transformations with a
greater efficiency than you can find anywhere in the
dumps: I mean, the quantity of structured mass you have

at the end is almost perfectly equal to that at the
beginning: on the dump, though, fire, efficient,
will achieve nothing but ash, heat, and smoke: excellent

100

change, but poor payload: or take rust, sluggish,
but it operates okay, not that you can do much with
ironic dust: the thing is to derive the *jus commune*

from the *jus singulare:* never must the *jus commune*
breeze through eradicating the *jus singulare:* the *jus
commune* must be merely a fall-out from happenstance:

that way it can find some curvature (if any) with the
actual: otherwise, the *jus commune* might become clear
to itself and propose imposition: never: never never:

101

I don't think I want to be buried here in these rocky
hills: once underground, how could I ever get my arms
free of the silk and steel, how could I ever with those

feet travel through the earth to my sweet home country
where all the flesh that bore me, back through grandfathers
and grandmothers, lies, and my little

brothers and my little sister I never saw, born before
me and dying small: and where will my living sisters
be put down, not here, and their children who might

102

visit me sometime to weep: but, a running weed,
I've come off up here and started a new offshoot
nucleus of a family and that sort of act perhaps should

be run into the ground: I mean, extended, preserved
into the ground: but this is phantasmagoria: death's
indifference will absorb living nostalgias and, anyway,

earth's a single mother and all who lie in her are brothers
and sisters: jungle cats and mudcats, sleek and slick:
the other night on Hee-Haw somebody said, "slick as

103

a mudcat's fin:" that's slick: poetry to the people,
not that they will ever acknowledge it: well, it's
night now and still fair, the moon full: the temperature

is dropping and the heater picking up: I put John's
tent together in the basement this afternoon: 8 rods
of fiberglass, connected with flexible tubes into 4

lengths, those then run through the sleeves, aluminum
sleeves adding support at the joints, and all brought
together at the top: a zipper door: his little house:

104

I looked up man in the dictionary and he was illustrated
and, as it turned out, chiefly muscle, a red fabric, and
bone, the whiteness men share: this creature, I

thought, has taken over, I know not whether because of
the freedom of the fingerbones or of the wagging, detachable
jaw, one about as gross and fine as the other: he

depends, ultimately, I thought again, on grass but, my,
what a transfiguration from the grass: he sees, his
vision air-clear: he tastes and feels: he thinks, ah:

105

he devours: he falls into necessities, or madnesses, only
his body can untangle: he carries in his lobed, zoned
skull earth's little supernova, the cerebral explosion,

somewhat in its stems and exfoliations like a mushroom
cloud: in him is ticking the californium 254 he's
detected in bombs and stars, whether still in its

first or some lesser half-life, unknown: but his little
explosion is growing up to equal celestial models: for
example, the other night the paper said two nearby

106

galaxies, hidden by our Milky Way, have been found, sight
having made other kinds of sight hunting, eating, loving
had no use for, some high conditions of burning: oh, yes,

we're *in* the explosions and we're going to see them out
and no other course could be half as interesting: falling
back can't help us now, returning to nature's lovely

subtle mechanisms: forward to the finish, of course, the
way it's always been or to a knowledge how to avoid the
finish: the possibility seen through to its perfect end:

107

the young are earnest, impatient: the older have learned
the alternatives, to be wrecked or reconciled: oh,
but it's not that easy: combinations and degrees make

life rough and rugged: yuck, yuck, the muck-sleet sings
pone the midnight windowpane, and the shattery wind
the shutters shudders: the confessor yanks up a belch

of privacy gone to seed: orangutans aren't groupy
as gorillas: cello alto solo pronto: if there is to be
no principle of inclusion, then, at least, there ought

108

to be a principle of exclusion, for to go with a maw at
the world as if to chew it up and spit
it out again as one's own is to trifle with terrible

affairs: I think I will leave out China, the perturbations
and continuities, transmutations and permutations of
Chinese civilization because, since that is so much,

giving it up's an immediate and cordial act of abasement,
betokening readiness to leave the world alone as
currently constituted (but, of course, how could words

109

do otherwise!): but I'm willing also to leave out most,
if not all, of the Amazon basin (all those trees, what
a whack), millions of islands I've never heard of and

some big ones I have, all ocean bottoms, all very high
places (whose spirituality blurs me), nearly all clouds
(which come and go lots before they pass through here), and,

if the population of the earth is four billion people,
then nearly four billion people: am I safe yet: of
course not: principles of exclusion become inclusive, etc.:

110

hiatuses, non-sequiturs, and indiligences later (nine hours
and forty-three minutes daylight) federal reorganizations
and revenue-sharings, advancings on extremely heavy

volume, what is everything about or anything for:
procedure's the only procedure: if things don't add
up, they must interest at every moment: a

difficulty: yesterday, severe, high-altitude winds
took our lower atmospheres in tow, making highly-compressed
bottom stirs, thunder at noon, one flash and blam,

111

and an even mixture of snow, rain, and sleet: zero
visibility was visible as near waves and white streams:
today is iron-fist windy and nudging zero: outside the

pheasant have lost all fear: they hunker down by the
picket fence, inattentive as the enemyless, or knowing
the enemy, too, must bear the cold: the ground is

assuming the curvatures of wind, flat-open places skinned
clean of snow, interruptions by fall-out being built up
to, mounds with sharp precipices, sometimes a mound

                                 1 1 2

breaking loose into strings of fast snow: I am unnerved
by openness and pure prose: the blue spruce is like
sprinkled with white crowsfeet, the inner intensive stems

branching, holding snow the needles can't: and into the
huge, round yew bush starlings light and go two-thirds
under: they peck the frit of snow the wind leaves

and drink: I'm reading Xenophon's *Oeconomicus* "with
considerable pleasure and enlightenment" and with
appreciation that saying so fills this stanza nicely.

Eyesight

It was May before my
attention came
to spring and

my word I said
to the southern slopes
I've

missed it, it
came and went before
I got right to see:

don't worry, said the mountain,
try the later northern slopes
or if

you can climb, climb
into spring: but
said the mountain

it's not that way
with all things, some
that go are gone

Left

Particularly near sundown
other worlds
    (dome on
dome)
suggest themselves to longing,

tangerine airs,
violets burnt out emeralds,

time's rush into wind sheet
as the sun nears the ridge,
a skinny plane slipping

at the last moment through
the thinnest rift and
away

where the sun locks
as with a melting opening
the exact high center

of another possibility—

the self-justifying delusions
of darkening,
this inscrutable by clarity
    & undifferentiation,

this single-centered single
dome

spent in the mind's-eye
gathering of peripheral sight.

The Arc Inside and Out
for Harold Bloom

If, whittler and dumper, gross carver
into the shadiest curvings, I took branch
and meat from the stalk of life, threw

away the monies of the treasured,
treasurable mind, cleaved memory free
of the instant, if I got right down

shucking off periphery after periphery
to the glassy vague gray parabolas
and swoops of unnailable perception,

would I begin to improve the purity,
would I essentialize out the distilled
form, the glitter-stone that whether

the world comes or goes clicks gleams
and chinks of truth self-making, never
to be shuttered, the face-brilliant core

stone: or if I, amasser, heap shoveler,
depth pumper, took in all springs and
oceans, paramoecia and moons, massive

buttes and summit slants, rooted trunks
and leafages, anthologies of wise words,
schemata, all grasses (including the

tidal *Spartinas*, marginal, salty
broadsweeps) would I finally come on a
suasion, large, fully-informed, restful

scape, turning back in on itself, its
periphery enclosing our system with
its bright dot and allowing in nonparlant

quantities at the edge void, void, and
void, would I then feel plenitude
brought to center and extent, a sweet

easing away of all edge, evil, and surprise:
these two ways to dream! dreaming them's
the bumfuzzlement—the impoverished

diamond, the heterogeneous abundance
starved into oneness: ultimately, either
way, which is our peace, the little

arc-line appears, inside which is nothing,
outside which is nothing—however big,
nothing beyond: however small, nothing

within: neither way to go's to stay, stay
here, the apple an apple with its own hue
or streak, the drink of water, the drink,

the falling into sleep, restfully ever the
falling into sleep, dream, dream, and
every morning the sun comes, the sun.

Index of First Lines